Witnessing Where You Live Work & Play

A Training Guide for Missional Living

Neal H. Creecy, Ph.D.

Witnessing
Where You
Live
Work
& Play

A Training Guide for Missional Living

HIS+RIA
CHRISTIAN

Histria Christian

Las Vegas ♦ Chicago ♦ Palm Beach

Published in the United States of America by
Histria Books
7181 N. Hualapai Way, Ste. 130-86
Las Vegas, NV 89166 U.S.A.
HistriaBooks.com

Histria Christian is an imprint of Histria Books dedicated to books that embody and promote Christian values and an understanding of the Christian faith. Titles published under the imprints of Histria Books are distributed worldwide.

Scripture quotations are from The ESV® Bible (The Holy Bible, English Standard Version®), © 2001 by Crossway, a publishing ministry of Good News Publishers. Used by permission. All rights reserved.

Library of Congress Control Number: 2024944153

ISBN 978-1-59211-515-0 (softcover)
ISBN 978-1-59211-527-3 (eBook)

Contents

Dedication

I am grateful for the opportunity to publish this book, which I hope will be used for God's glory in expanding His Kingdom here on earth. I would like to offer three dedications for this book.

First, I would like to dedicate this book to two men who had a profound impact on me in ministry. Dr. Clayton Cloer and Frank Porter. These two men invested in a young sixteen-year-old boy who had surrendered to ministry. I am so grateful for their influence and friendship throughout the years.

Second, I would like to dedicate this book to my seminary professors at Mid-America Baptist Theological Seminary. Having done both my MDiv and Ph.D. at Mid-America, the professors there invested so much into me. I am grateful for their faithful service to the Lord, their scholarship, and for the training I received that still impacts my ministry today.

Third, I would like to dedicate this book to my parents, James and Marshall Lea Creecy. My parents sacrificed so much for my sister Kelley and me. I think their greatest gift to us was releasing us to follow God's call to ministry, even when it spread us across the world. They were always supportive and encouraging. While they are greatly missed, their legacy of faith continues to bear fruit.

Preface

One of the greatest privileges of my life has been the opportunity to train people in how to share their faith. There is so much joy in seeing people equipped, mobilized, and sent out for the Gospel. Because of this, I was so grateful for the opportunity to publish a book that will hopefully help people know how to witness and help them implement strategies to begin living missionally where they live, work, and play.

Solomon wrote that there is nothing new under the sun. That is very true when it comes to this book. What I have tried to do is take thirty years of what I have learned through reading, training, listening to other practitioners, and my own experience and put it all together in a training book that equips people to know how to share their faith and how to develop ministry platforms where they can begin reaching lost people with the Gospel.

There are three main parts to this book. The first deals with understanding your calling as a witness. I seek to address unproductive mindsets that have taken root within Western Christianity that limit the number of Christians who actively and regularly engage in evangelism. The second part teaches you how to witness. There are many great methods and tools available to teach you how to witness. The method I teach is based on what I have been taught and what I have found works well for me. It teaches you how to share your faith through using your own personal testimony as well as how to walk someone through the Bible to understand salvation. The third section teaches you how to develop ministry strategies for the three domains where we live our lives – first, second, and third spaces (where you live, work, and play).

A goal of this book is to not only help people be regularly involved in evangelism, but to show there are other strategies than just door-to-door witnessing. I am not at all against door-to-door witnessing, but it is not the only way. For several years of my Christian life, I only saw evangelism through the lens of wide seed sowing of the Gospel that takes place in door-to-door witnessing. While this is a needed model, I have also come to realize that developing platforms for witnessing that are centered around intentional relationship building with lost people can be effective in impacting lost people. I have also greater success in discipling believers who came to faith through relationship than those who I met in door-to-door style evangelism. If, however, you are active in wide seed sowing of the Gospel, let me encourage you to continue spreading the Gospel far and wide. This book is not to give you strategies that compete with your model, but to complement it.

A second goal of this book is to help people rethink church. In most contexts, the local church campus should not be the primary place of evangelism. Pastors should not be the primary ones leading people to Christ. Everyday Christians should be the primary people leading lost people to Jesus. As they go about their day, living, working, and playing in the community, they should be investing in the lives of lost people and leading them to Jesus.

I hope this book helps you in your journey as a witness for Jesus. I pray that it may encourage you, equip you, and assist you in becoming a Christian who takes the Great Commission of Jesus seriously. May the Lord bless you as you seek to know Him more and to make Him known.

Chapter 1
Words Matter

Have you ever been sitting on your couch on a Saturday morning and heard a knock at the door? You open the door expecting to find some guy selling solar and it is two young men dressed in white shirts, both with name tags that have "Elder" in front of their names. Your local Mormon missionaries are out and about wanting to talk to you about Jesus. Most people that I know simply tell them they are not interested and close the door. Some Christians, however, engage the missionaries in a conversation about Jesus and salvation. What these Christians find is that the Mormon missionaries use a lot of the same words that we use. They will talk about God the Father, Jesus, the Holy Spirit, being saved, and the Word of God. Mormons will even tell you that they are Christians. I remember one time I was sitting with two Mormon missionaries, and they told me that the words "Christian" and "Mormon" are synonymous.

It is not uncommon for Christians to be confused by Mormons because they use the same terms we use. It is a technique I like to call "term switching." Term switching is where you use the same words as someone else, but a different dictionary. When a Mormon says that he believes in Jesus, it is a very different Jesus than the Bible. The Jesus he believes in was created, lived as a man, and was exalted, which means he became a god. This is very different from the Jesus of the Bible. When Mormons say that they are saved, it means that they can begin the process of moving towards exultation. Again, this is very different than what the Bible teaches about salvation. An important lesson to learn when speaking to Mormons is to make sure they define their terms. Words matter. The meaning of words matters.

Just like words matter when it comes to witnessing to Mormons, words also matter in us understanding the Bible. There are four words related to the topic of witnessing in the Bible that many Christians either do not fully understand, or they have a completely wrong understanding of them.

Church

What is a church? While this may seem like a simple question, it is one that can create a good deal of debate. Missiologists (those who study missions) have written much literature debating what is and what is not a church. If you ask your everyday Christians to define a church, you may get a slew of answers. For some, the church is the building where they meet. For others, they will tell you that the church is made up of the people.

While the purpose of this book is not to write an exhaustive treatise on what the church is, I think it is important to clarify what the church is and why it exists. Understanding what the Bible teaches about the church is important for believers to understand why their engagement in evangelism is so important. The best place to look for clarity on this issue is the first place the word church is used in the New Testament – Matthew 16:18 – "And I tell you, you are Peter, and on this rock I will build my church, and the gates of hell shall not prevail against it."

This passage answers the two questions of what is the church and what is its purpose? First, Jesus says that He is going to build His church. Baker Encyclopedia of the Bible defines church as: "A group or assembly of persons called together for a particular purpose."[1] The reason for this definition is because of the word used in the original language of the New Testament, Greek, which is *ekklesia*. This was a common word in New Testament times. For example, it was used to speak of legislative bodies. Groups of people who were called out from the population for the purpose of creating laws to govern the people.[2] *Ekklesia* can also be used to describe a more casual assembly of people, or a gathering of people of like belief. The primary meaning of the word is a group of people called out to accomplish a particular task. The context of this verse requires us to take the primary meaning because Jesus immediately articulates why the people have been gathered – to engage the kingdom of hell in battle.

After Jesus stated that He would build His church, He then gave a promise that shows us the purpose of the church. He said that "the gates of hell shall not prevail

---

[1] Walter A. Elwell and Barry J. Beitzel, "Church," *Baker Encyclopedia of the Bible* (Grand Rapids, MI: Baker Book House, 1988), 458.

[2] William Arndt et al., *A Greek-English Lexicon of the New Testament and Other Early Christian Literature* (Chicago: University of Chicago Press, 2000), 303.

against it." Here, Jesus uses military language to show that we are in a battle against hell. An important detail to note is that gates are defensive. That means we are to be on the offense storming the gates of hell in the name of Jesus. Too many churches have adopted a defensive stance when it comes to reaching the world. Too many Christians and churches have replaced the Great Commission of "go ye" with a "come y'all" strategy. For many churches, the primary place people are saved is in the weekend worship service. The church either passively waits for people to show up to hear the Gospel, or they actively try to attract lost people to their services. Either way, they are not going out and reaching lost people, but are primarily only reaching lost people that happen to attend their services. You do not overcome gates by waiting for them to come to you, but rather, you go to them and break through to achieve victory.

Now there is much more that can be said about all that a church does. The New Testament has a lot more to say about how a church functions, its calling to make disciples, how it is to be organized, and how it is to care for its members. The point I want to make here is that when Jesus introduced the idea that He was going to build a church, he emphasized that it would be a called-out group of people with a primary purpose of engaging in battle against hell. This means that as we understand how a church should operate, and what priorities a church should have, we should see ourselves as a military unit working to destroy hell. Not through physical violence, as that is not what God has called us to do, but through sharing the Gospel.

So why is understanding what a church is and why it exists so important? The reason is because if we do not understand what we are and why we exist, then we will never be effective in what God has called us to do. There are many examples I can give as to how it is obvious that many Christians and churches have lost sight on what a church is supposed to be. Let me give you a few examples.

Having been in full-time ministry for almost thirty years, and most of those years in a pastoral role, I have talked to many people about why they joined a particular church. Some have told me they joined their church because it had good preaching. Some because of the type of music in the worship service. Others joined because of a strong youth or children's ministry. All of these answers have one thing in common – the person I spoke to joined a particular church based on what he or she would get out of it. This reveals that many people believe that the primary purpose of a church is to serve its members. This has led to a practice where churches schedule so many activities that its members do not have any time left-over to be involved in activities outside of the church.

A second example is that most service opportunities in churches are focused on serving the congregation instead of getting off the church campus and reaching the lost. We have ushers, small group leaders, leadership teams of various kinds, parking attendants, children and youth workers, choir members, tech teams, and many other positions that serve the body. If someone is serving in one of these areas, we consider them to be faithful. It doesn't matter that very few, if any, of our members are regularly sharing their faith and leading people to Jesus. Now, it is true that many people in the military, even during a war, are not on the front lines. They are serving in support rolls to allow the combat soldiers to engage the enemy in battle. I understand that there are service roles that are important, needed roles for the church to function and be healthy. The problem is that many churches do not have any significant "combat soldiers" that are engaging lostness outside of the church campus. A military that never leaves base will never conquer new terri-tory.

Though I could continue listing other examples to show that many Christians and churches really do not understand what they are and why they exist, I will give one more. Once I was speaking to a pastor friend of mine. He is the founding pastor of the church he serves and has seen significant growth over the past several years. He has recently had some of his long-time members begin to talk about leaving or suggesting that the church stop trying to reach people so they can focus on their members. Statements have been made like, "I used to know everyone and now I don't know half of the people here." Throughout the years, I've heard so many stories of church fights that were centered on the church growing and people not liking it. Church planting and church growth experts will tell you that a church that is planted and grows to a significant number will lose most of their founding members through the process. This is because the church no longer feels like home. They no longer know everyone. The pastor doesn't have the same amount of time to spend with them. New people are having input into the direction of the church. While I understand why people feel this way, it reveals that they do not really understand the nature of the church. Can you imagine an army being upset that they are winning the war? That is exactly what is happening when people are upset that a church is reaching too many people. They don't understand that the purpose of the church is to win the spiritual war God has called us to fight. This attitude also reveals an underlying current that sees the church as an organization that primarily exists to serve the members over accomplishing the mission.

As I previously stated, I could give you many more examples of how churches and Christians have lost touch with what the church is and why it exists. The question now is: "How does this impact you?" Has this chapter challenged you in your view of the church? Are you an advocate at your church for staying focused on the mission of reaching the lost? Do you embrace new people? Have you been on the front lines reaching lost people with the Gospel? Do you have an attitude that leads you to examine what you are adding to the church as opposed to being primarily concerned with what the church does for you? Are you willing to lay your comfort at the alter to see the mission accomplished?

Let me close this section with a word of encouragement from the passage we examined. Don't ever forget the promise in the statement Jesus made – we win. The gates of hell will not prevail. The only way for the gates of hell to win is for the church to remain at base camp and refuse to bust the gates in and see people saved. One day the war will be over, the victory will have been won, and God's army, the church, will gather around their King and spend eternity celebrating Him.

Holy

The word "holy" is often thrown around in Christian circles. We talk about God being holy. We talk about the need for us, as followers of Jesus, to be holy. I don't think, however, that many Christians have a thorough understanding of what it means to be holy. For them, something is either holy or unholy (profane). In the Jewish mindset, however, things were categorized in three categories – holy, common, or profane. Something that is holy is something that has been set apart or consecrated for God. So, there are two concepts that we need to unpack to understand what it means to be holy. The first is that we are to be set apart for God. The second is that there are three categories, as mentioned above, that people or things can fall into when it comes to holiness.

In my years of pastoring, I have found that many Christians view holiness as a list of dos and don'ts as opposed to foundationally being about your purpose. Furthermore, the greatest emphasis is usually on the don'ts. For example, the old saying, "Don't drink, don't chew, don't date girls that do." For many Christians, holiness is about what you don't do. While it is true that you cannot live a holy life while engaging in willful sin at the same time, holiness is more about your purpose than it is your actions. If you truly have the right purpose and motivation, your actions will follow. If, however, you have the wrong purpose or motivation, then you are missing the mark on what it means to be holy. Holiness that is divorced from the right purpose and motivation is reduced to moralism. I have found many Christians that have fallen into the trap of moralism instead of living a holy life. Let me give you an example. Picture a teenager in your church that obeys his parents, does well in school, is polite, goes to church without a fuss, and is not out there getting drunk or being disorderly with his friends. Many within the church would say, "What a godly young man." They would declare that he is living a holy life. The problem with this assessment is that the conclusion is based on outward actions of morality and not necessarily holiness. Let's take this same young man that everyone thinks is holy. After further investigation you find out that he never reads the Bible, he never spends time in prayer, he only does some of the spiritual disciplines when prompted by his parents or fellow church members. Is he truly holy or just moral? You see, holiness is not primarily about what you do, but understanding your purpose. Holiness is understanding that you have been set apart from the world for God so that you may know Him and glorify His name. If someone says he is holy, yet he doesn't seek God in relationship, then he really is not holy. He may be moral by religious standards, but that doesn't make him holy. Now let me be clear, if a guy says he is walking in relationship with God, but he habitually, and unrepentantly lives a life contrary to the Word of God, he isn't holy. True holiness will transform how you live. Moralism, however, only gives an appearance of holiness, but isn't true holiness.

The second concept we need to examine is the understanding of the three categories. Again, in the Jewish mindset, things were either holy, common, or profane. Things that were holy were to be set apart for the use of worshiping God. Things that were common were things that everyone could use. Things that were profane were dirty or defiled. During Jesus' day, they would have had dishes that fell in all three categories. There were dishes that were consecrated as holy. They were only to be used in temple worship. There were dishes that were common. These would have been in people's homes. Anyone could eat from them. There were also dishes that would have been considered profane. What made something profane? Something was considered profane if it was forbidden or had been in contact with something forbidden. This brings up something important to understand. If something that was supposed to be holy was treated as common, it made it profane. If a dish that was supposed to be used only for temple worship was used at the supper table, it was now profane and no longer fit for being used in the temple. The best example I've ever heard about how treating something holy as common makes it profane came from my good friend, Dr. Clayton Cloer. A toothbrush is to be holy unto you. That means that it is set apart for only you to use. Imagine if your toothbrush was passed around and used by everyone. How would you feel when it came back to you? Disgusted? That is the answer I normally get. You see, when an item is supposed to be holy, but is treated as common, it actually makes it profane.

So why am I spending time unpacking the issue of holiness in a witness training and strategy book? The reason is because of what happens when the two concepts we just examined come together. I think one of the reasons so few Christians in the West share their faith on a regular basis is because many Christians are not living a holy life. I don't think it is because they don't want to live a holy life, but rather, they don't know what it really means. They are living lives of moralism instead of holy lives. They are following a list of dos and don'ts, but they have not understood that they have been set apart to live a passionate life for God. A life that is focused on knowing Jesus and glorifying His name throughout the world. Because these people understand holiness two-dimensionally, either holy or profane, they believe they are living holy lives because they are not out there living in open sin. They aren't cheating on their spouses. They aren't stealing. They aren't murdering. They, therefore, must be living a holy life because they are not living a profane life.

The problem with this two-dimensional view of holiness, is that many Christians do not realize that while they are not necessarily living a profane life, they are living a common life. Throughout the years I have noticed that most of my church members have the same dreams and aspirations as the lost people around them. They are focused on having nice homes, increasing their wealth, providing a great childhood for their children, and putting away for retirement. None of these things are intrinsically profane. The problem, however, is that they are common. We have not been called to live common lives, but rather, holy lives. We should wake up every morning with a desire to know Jesus more and to glorify His name throughout the world. That means glorifying His name in our home. That means glorifying His name at work or school. That means glorifying His name in every activity we do. There should be a clear distinction between believers and lost people. If the people in your community were asked to describe what you are most passionate about, would their answer be that you are passionate about Jesus. I think too many Christians are known as church goers as opposed to being known as people who are passionate about knowing Jesus and glorifying His name.

I hope this section causes you to evaluate your life. Have you simply been living a moral life, or have you been living a holy life? You may be thinking, "What does it look like to passionately live to know Jesus and glorify His name?" To answer this, I would encourage you to think about how people express their passion for other things. Many people are passionate about sports. In 2023, the Las Vegas Golden Knights won the NHL Stanley Cup. I love the Knights! I watch the games. I talk to other people about the team. I proudly wear VGK apparel. I read articles about the team. Think about how a young man acts when he is passionately in love with a girl. He wants to spend time with her, he spends money on her, he talks to her, he tells his friends about her. He priorities his time around her. He thinks about her constantly. These are all manifestations of his passion for her. Do any of these descriptions describe your relationship with Jesus? If you are truly passionate about Jesus it will spill over into your speech. It will affect your schedule, your money, and every other aspect of your life.

If, after evaluating your life, you feel that you have fallen into moralism instead of holiness. If you recognize that you are living a common life instead of a holy life, then the simple solution is to repent. God has called you to live a holy life. Not doing so is to live in disobedience to Him. Go to the Lord, confess that you are not living the holy life He has called you to live. Receive His forgiveness. Ask Him to grow your passion for Him. You cannot change yourself, but you can surrender to and call upon Jesus to change you and He will.

Witness

Earlier, I talked about the technique utilized by people like the Mormons called term switching. It is where you use the same words, but a different dictionary. I don't think there is a single word that the Western church has used term switching against more than the word witness. I remember when I was in college, a slogan became popular. "Share Jesus, use words if necessary." Christians started wearing t-shirts with this slogan. They bought bumper stickers and placed them on their cars. The problem with this slogan is that it is thoroughly unbiblical.

I think the best passage for us to understand the Biblical concept of witness is Acts 1:8 – "But you will receive power when the Holy Spirit has come upon you, and you will be my witnesses in Jerusalem and in all Judea and Samaria, and to the end of the earth." There are four things I want you to see in this text.

1. What does it mean to witness?

This verse tells us what we are to do. That is, witness. While this seems so simple, many people are confused on what it means to be a witness. On more than one occasion, I have had a Christian tell me that the way he witnesses is by how he lives his life. The question is, "Is that really a witness?" My answer would be no. So, what is a witness? It is important that we understand that this word is a legal term. For someone to be a witness he must meet two criteria. First, he must have first-hand knowledge. Before I was saved, I could not be a witness for Jesus. I had heard that Jesus saves. I had heard that he could change peoples' lives. But I hadn't experienced it. I did not have first-hand knowledge. However, after I was saved, I could be a witness because I had experienced His saving power. I had experienced the change that He brought to my life.

Second, a witness must bear testimony about what he has seen or heard. It would be ludicrous for a man to put on a suit, go to a court of law, swear to tell the truth, and then sit there and expect to not say anything. You can't simply look like a witness; to be a witness you must give testimony. Now, let me clarify something. How you live your life is important. If an opposing attorney cannot contradict your testimony, he will try to attack your credibility. He will try to convince the court that you are not trustworthy. That your witness cannot be believed. How a Christian lives his life is important. It establishes his credibility as a witness. I remember one night I was in Walmart and ran into a guy who was in my Sunday School class. He was with a friend. I started witnessing to his friend, telling him about how Jesus could save him and change his life. The problem, however, is that the guy with him, who attended Sunday School with me, was drunk. He kept interjecting telling his friend how he needed to listen. How important this was. I could see the look of disgust in his friend's eyes. He didn't want to hear from his friend about how Jesus changes lives when his friend was standing next to him drunk. The guy had no credibility as a witness. This illustrates how important it is to live a holy life before lost people. It is not because how you live your life is your witness, but rather, it establishes your credibility as a witness. People are more open to hear the Gospel when they can see how it has impacted your life in a positive way. They still, however, must hear the Gospel to be saved.

2. Where are we to witness?

This passage also tells us where we are to be witnesses. I am not going to spend a lot of time on this, as the focus of this book is on reaching your Jerusalem, but it is worth noting that we should seek to see Jesus glorified throughout the world. Jesus lists four places we will be His witnesses. First, he says Jerusalem. That would be the city or town where you live. Second, he says Judea. That would be your nation. Third, he says Samaria. Some have taken this to mean the countries next door to you. That may be the case, but I think it could also have another meaning. It could mean that you go to your enemies. The Jews hated the Samaritans. Even our enemies need Jesus. Fourth, and finally, he says to the end of the earth. We still have much work to do. Almost a third of the world still does not have the Gospel.

Let me say one final word about where we witness before I move on to how we witness. Some people believe that the emphasis of Acts 1:8 puts the different locations in order. Because of this, I've had Christians ask me why should we spend money on missions when there are still so many lost people here in the United States? In the Greek, the emphasis is not sequential, but contemporaneous. That means we are to be involved in all locations at the same time. We see this modeled in the New Testament. The believers did not wait for all of Jerusalem to be reached before they started heading to other parts of the world to share the Gospel. Our churches should be a part of reaching our towns and cities, our countries, our enemies, and the ends of the earth for the glory of God.

3. How do we witness?

With this question I do not mean to ask what method of witnessing we use. There are many different methods to sharing the Gospel. I present one in this book. What I mean by this question is by what power do we witness? Do we witness according to our own speaking ability, or our own power to save someone? Of course not. We witness by the power of the Holy Spirit.

My first year as a seminary student working on a Master of Divinity degree was a challenging year. It was during that year that I started taking New Testament Greek. My professor that year was Dr. David Shackelford. He was a good professor, but a hard one. Greek did not come easily for me, as learning a language is a lot of straight memorizations. I can learn concepts quickly, but I've always struggled with memorizing. Almost every morning we would have a quiz. I would work on my Greek homework until midnight, and then get up at 5:00am so I could have another hour or so to study some more before class. I remember taking my first final in that class. There was no need for a study guide, because every vocabulary word and every paradigm that had been covered that term was on the test. I remember having a nightmare the night before the test. I was taking the test and then it started multiplying and spinning in the air. It was like the test was chasing me. I am grateful for that year and all that I learned because it opened the Scriptures to me in a way that I had never experienced.

There were times while studying Greek that I would be about ready to give up and quit. It seemed like whenever I was ready to throw in the towel, that Dr. Shackelford would stop the lesson and say, "Brothers, this is why knowing Greek matters." He would then show us how our understanding of Greek could give us greater clarity on a passage. It was on one such occasion that he showed us the significance of Acts 1:8. You see, there is more than one word in Greek that is translated into the English word "power." Two such words are *exousia and dynamis*. These two words are synonyms that can both be translated power in English. They do, however, have different emphases. *Exousia* emphasizes the power to do something because you have the authority. It sometimes is translated as "authority." If you ready Matthew 28:18 in the New American Standard Bible, it renders *exousia* as authority. Some things you have the power to do because you have the authority to do them. *Dynamis*, however, does not speak of authority, but rather of ability. You could translate Acts 1:8: "you will receive ability when the Holy Spirit comes upon you, and you will be my witnesses . . ." Jesus was saying that we would be given the ability to witness. This is so important. I remember having a conversation with a church member one night following a witness training class. This church member seemed so defeated. He told me that he just couldn't witness. He did not believe he had the ability. What he didn't understand, is that he was unintentionally calling Jesus a liar. Jesus promised that we would receive the ability to be His witnesses. We do not witness based on our own ability, but by the ability that God has promised to give us. Part of being a good witness is recognizing that you can't do it in your own strength, but God has promised to empower you to do it.

When I was sixteen, I met a man named Ronnie. Ronnie was in his mid to late forties when I first met him. He suffered from a mild intellectual disability. He was considered high functioning, but his condition limited him in many ways. He lived by himself, but his family had to oversee his business affairs. He could work, but it had to be a simple job. He was employed by the local Sonic drive-in to clean the parking lot each morning. Because of his condition, he was extremely socially unaware. He attended the local church that we had joined. The church made him sit in the very back row. It wasn't because they were trying to be mean, but because if someone was sitting behind Ronnie he would turn around and in a loud voice start preaching to them in the middle of the sermon. What he lacked in social awareness, he made up in having the most amazing memory. He had most of the Bible memorized. He also could quote you just about any baseball or football statistic you could ever ask for. He could give you play-by-play of World Series games that had taken place years before. It was amazing to see the power of his brain in memorization. The other thing about Ronnie is that he could talk. As my dad use to say, "He could talk the horns off a brass billy goat."

I remember one day I was at the local Chinese buffet and low and behold Ronnie walked in. He loved the Chinese buffet. He saw me and walked right up to me. As we were moving down the buffet, Ronnie was talking a mile a minute. He was telling me that he had led a young lady to Christ. He went on to say that he thought it was going to be a shut-out year, but he finally led someone to Christ this year. He told me that he had gone nine years without a shut-out. Now, I am not proud to say this, but I was not in the mood that day to listen to Ronnie. Once he started talking, he would not stop. I was busy thinking that I couldn't take him talking the entire lunch. But as he was telling me that he had gone nine years without a shut-out year, I felt as if the Lord said to me: "I'll use him because he is willing." I can't tell you the amount of conviction that washed over me. I also wondered how many of the church members could say they had gone nine years without a shut-out year. Here was Ronnie, a mentally retarded, socially inept man that most people tried to avoid, yet he had led someone to Jesus nine years in a row. It showed me that what Jesus said was true - He would give us the ability. Can you say that you have gone nine years without a shut-out? Can you imagine how your church would grow if everyone in the church was faithful to share the Gospel and everyone had nine years without a shut-out? Jesus has given you the ability to share, the question is, are you willing?

4. What is the cost of witnessing?

Etymology is the study of how words came into being and how their meaning changes throughout time. Language is not static, but rather, it is constantly changing as the meaning of words change. A few years ago, a pastor friend of mine posted a picture of his son, who was around twelve years old at the time, wearing a pair of new shoes. My friend had made some sort of smart comment to his son about the shoes. His son responded by saying, "Respect the drip, Karen." What I found hilarious about the post was all the comments that followed. Someone asked what that phrase meant. Then there were several people trying to figure out exactly what the boy was trying to say. It sounded like I was in a nursing home community room full of senior citizens trying to figure out what in the world this boy had just said. They understood each word in the sentence, but they didn't understand what the sentence meant. Why? Because some of the meanings of the words have changed. Drip no longer just means the falling of small drops of water, but it can also mean that an article of clothing is extremely stylish. Karen is no longer just a common name for a woman, but it is now a slang term for a middle-aged woman who overreacts to a situation and is hating on someone. It is tough to be named Karen these days.

The reason for the short lesson on etymology is because the etymology of the word witness is important for us in the discussion of what it costs to be a witness. The Greek word that is translated witness is the word *martys*. As previously mentioned, it was a legal term that described someone who gave first-hand testimony of something he had seen or heard. Throughout time, however, the word also came to mean someone who was killed because of his testimony of Jesus. That is why the English word martyr etymologically comes from the Greek word *martys*. The connection between witnessing for Jesus and persecution became so prevalent that the word witness came to also mean someone who died for Jesus.

Back in the early 2000s, I was sitting in a training seminar on persecution led by Nik Ripkin. Nik had done unprecedented research on the persecuted church throughout the world. His findings provided major insights into how to operate as missionaries in persecuted areas. He later wrote a book and produced a movie on his research, both entitled *The Insanity of God*. I highly recommend both to you. Nik found that Christians throughout the world faced many forms of persecution. Some were denied medical care. Some were denied education for their children. Some were beaten, imprisoned, and tortured. Some lost their jobs and homes. Some Christian parents had to choose to renounce Christ or lose custody of their children. Finally, some were killed.

In all the areas of the world Nik studied, he found a common denominator between Christians and persecution. It didn't matter if you were facing persecution in communist China or the Islamic Middle East. That common denominator was witnessing and persecution. Most of the time, if Christians did not witness, they did not face persecution. As long as they remained silent, they would usually be left alone. Through his research, Nik realized that the goal of persecutors was not primarily to hurt, imprison, or kill Christians, but rather, to silence them. Most persecution never progresses further than threats. That is because threats are often enough to silence Christians.

Have you ever wondered why there isn't more persecution of Christians in America? Some would say it is because we are a country founded by Christian principles. Others would point to our constitution and remind us that we believe in religious freedom. While those two things may have contributed to a lack of persecution in America, I think there is another reason. I once heard a prominent leader of the Southern Baptist Convention state that he believed nine out of ten

Southern Baptists never share their faith. This should have been shocking to me. Southern Baptists are known for being a missionary and evangelistic denomination. How could nine out of ten Southern Baptists never share their faith? Sadly, I was not surprised by the statement. I don't know if this leader had done a proper study to come to this statistic, but in my experience in Southern Baptist churches for almost thirty years, it is probably true. As I learned from Nik Ripkin years ago, there is no need for persecution in the United States because the church has already been silenced.

The reality for followers of Jesus, is that if we are obedient to His command for us to witness, we will eventually face persecution. In the West, the most that Christians have had to endure is ridicule. As the West grows in its rejection of Jesus, greater forms of persecution may come. The question is whether we will allow fear of persecution keep us from being obedient to our Lord. I am reminded of what Jim Elliot, the famous missionary and martyr that served and died in Ecuador, once said: "He is no fool who gives what he cannot keep to gain what he cannot lose." Let us not be ashamed in the presence of our Lord because we were afraid to be witnesses for Him.

Pastor

The fourth and final word that I want us to examine is the word pastor. It may seem strange for you that I would want to examine what a pastor is. You may be thinking that everyone knows what a pastor is. The question is, do you really understand what their role should primarily be in evangelism? I believe that when you look at the majority of churches' evangelism strategies, the primary place where people get saved is in the weekly worship service. That means that the pastor is the primary person that does the evangelism for the church. While that may be the practice of many churches, is it a biblical model? Does having the pastor as the primary person of evangelism in a church follow the Biblical model of evangelism? To answer these questions, I want to look at Ephesians 4:11-12 – "[11] And he gave the apostles, the prophets, the evangelists, the shepherds and teachers, [12] to equip the saints for the work of ministry, for building up the body of Christ"

In the above passage, Paul gives a list of different roles in the church, one of which is shepherds. The term shepherd is what we know as pastor. The passage tells us two things about the pastor. First, we see that the pastor is a gift to the church. It says that he, speaking of Jesus, gave these different people to the church. A gift from God is something that should be held in high honor. Second, we see that Jesus had an intended use for pastors. Pastors, along with the other servants listed in the passage, were to equip the saints for the work of the ministry. This means that the primary role of the pastor is to equip saints to do the work of the ministry. Many churches believe it is the pastor's job to do the work of the ministry. While the pastor is to be involved in evangelism, as Paul told Timothy in 2 Timothy 4:5, he should not be the primary or only person sharing the Gospel. The problem is that in most of the churches I have known, he is the one expected to be sharing the Gospel on a regular basis, not the church members.

In 2024, Las Vegas had the privilege of hosting the Super Bowl. A pastor friend of mine sent me a text telling me he had a small favor to ask. I told him okay. He said it is just a tiny, small favor. Again, I said okay. He replied that it really was a teensy-weensy request. I finally told him to spit it out. He started to explain that the Super Bowl was a few months away and that he is a San Francisco 49ers fan. The 49ers were looking like they might make it to the Super Bowl. Finally, he asked if they made it to the Super Bowl, did I have any connections to get him a free ticket? I just laughed out loud when I read that text. Small request my foot! I have been offered tickets to the Vegas Golden Knights, The Las Vegas Raiders, the Formula One Race, and to many different concerts over the years. I've never, ever had anyone say to me: "You know, I have this extra ticket to the Super Bowl that I can't do anything with; would you like it?" The average price for the Super Bowl in Las Vegas was $8,600 per ticket. Some tickets were going as high as $37,000. Needless to say, when the 49ers made it to the Super Bowl, I got a text from my friend letting me know how disappointed he was in me that I did not come through for him with a ticket and that he was reduced to watching the game on his tv in his living room. I replied: "Where there is a fee, there's a remedy."

Now imagine if you had paid somewhere between $8,600 and $37,000 for a ticket to the game. You get to the stadium, made another financial investment in some snacks, and then finally got to your seat. You're so excited about the game. Your team is playing for the championship! As you sit waiting for the game to start, an announcement is made over the speaker. "Ladies and gentlemen, welcome to the 2024 Super Bowl, hosted in fabulous Las Vegas, Nevada. Today we have a special surprise for all of you. Instead of the players playing to determine the champion, the players are going to sit on the sidelines while the coaches from each team play each other. Enjoy the game!" You start to laugh, thinking that it is a joke. Suddenly, the teams enter the field. You notice that none of the players have helmets or are wearing pads. Then you notice chairs lined up on each side of the field. The players all go and sit in the chairs. Then, here comes another group of people onto the field. This group is in full pads and are carrying helmets. Some of the members of the group are old. Some look like it has been a decade or two since they worked out. There are some younger guys, but they sure look small. You start to realize the announcement wasn't a joke, but that the coaching staff from both teams are about to play each other. How mad would you be? You paid all this money to see the best in the world play, and now you have to watch a bunch of people who have never played NFL football, or at best is a has been. Can you imagine the outcry from the fans?

Now, as crazy as the above story is, this is exactly what we are doing in our churches. We are expecting the coaches to play the game instead of the players. Imagine a war where the generals are the ones on the front lines instead of the young, strong men and women who are the infantry soldiers? We would say that is a crazy strategy. I have learned in my years of pastoring that there are many people who are much better than I am in evangelism. I've had people that I have trained reach many more folks with the Gospel than I ever have. They had the gifting from God, they just needed the training and equipping from their pastors.

Do you see your pastors as the primary players or the coaches? Do you see your pastors as the generals or the frontline infantry soldiers? If you are a pastor, or a pastor in training reading this book, I want you to understand your God given role. You should lead your congregations to understand that they are the ones who are to go out there and win the battle. They are the ones who are gifted to be the primary witnesses to a lost world. Your job is to train and equip them. If you are a church member reading this book, don't miss out on the great work God has created you to do. Don't sit on the sidelines missing out on the blessings of leading people to Jesus. Get in the game! Get on the battlefield!

Putting Words into Action

In this chapter we have examined four words – church, holy, witness, and pastor. We have learned that the church is a group of people who have been called out to be part of a spiritual military unit with the objective of charging forward to defeat the gates of hell. We have learned that we are not to live common lives, but rather holy lives. Lives that are passionately focused on knowing Jesus and glorifying His name. We have learned that being a witness is not simply living out a good life in front of your neighbors, but actively testifying about Jesus. Finally, we have learned that our pastors are not to be the primary ones doing the work of evangelism, but rather they are to equip the church members so that they can do the work of the ministry.

Before you move on to the next chapter, let me encourage you to reflect on what you have learned in this chapter. As you examine your own understanding of these words and your own life, what needs to change? Does your thinking need to change? Do your actions need to change? Let me challenge you to take a minute and write down some next steps that will start you on the road to being the witness God has called you to be. Maybe you need to ask your pastor to train you in evangelism so you can do the work of the ministry. Maybe you need to start your day asking God to use you as His witness. Maybe you need to make a commitment to know Jesus more – to be consistent in spending time with Him each day. It is so easy to read a book like this and then not change anything in your life. Reflect, write down some action steps, share those steps with a brother or sister in Christ so that they can hold you accountable, and start moving in the direction God is calling you.

Let me close this chapter with a testimonial. When I was sixteen, I was a freshman in college and had just publicly surrendered to ministry. I had an opportunity to go on my first mission trip. Our church flew to Detroit, Michigan to lead a witness training seminar at a church in a suburb of Detroit. The church that we were working with had a big facility but had a small congregation. In times past, the church had grown to several hundred people. They were like a number of Southern Baptist churches in the North that had enjoyed larger congregations. The problem is that these churches had not reached northerns, but rather southern transplants who had moved from the South for jobs in the automotive industry. When the factories started closing, many of the southerners moved back to the

South and the churches dwindled in size. This church was slowly dying. It had been so long, and it was so rare to see anyone baptized, that they had started using the baptismal pool for storage.

The schedule for the week was intense. Our team spent three to four hours in prayer each morning. We would then have lunch together before heading out to spend three hours witnessing in the community. We went to parks, malls, anywhere we could find people to share the Gospel. We would then come back to the church, have an early dinner, and then lead a three-hour session on witness training. On the last full day, we took the members of the host church out with us to put into practice what they had learned about witnessing.

God moved in an amazing way that week. The relationships I formed with my church on that trip were deeper than any I had ever had in church. Anyone who has served in war will tell you that the bond you build with your fellow soldiers amid the battles are some of the strongest you will ever experience. We also had the joy of seeing multiple people come to faith during our days out witnessing. The greatest movement of God, however, is what He did in the life of that church. The thirty or so people who attended the training really caught the passion to share the Gospel. They became faithful in sharing the Gospel in their community and started seeing people saved. I heard a report six months later that the church had cleared out the baptismal pool. It was no longer used for storage, but for baptisms. Furthermore, instead of baptism being something that was rare, it was now a regular part of their services. It is a great testimony of how God will use a church if its members get serious about obedience to God's calling to be witnesses. Also, I can only imagine the joy and life that was breathed into that church. I'm sure it was exciting to show up every Sunday for worship and instead of sitting in a dying congregation, to be in a place and worship the Lord in celebration as week after week people's lives were transformed. That is the type of church I want to be a part of!

Chapter 2
Witnessing
Using Your Personal Testimony

The Soul Winner's Notebook

When I was sixteen years old, my family and I moved to Senatobia, Mississippi. The months leading up to the move had been quite difficult. My dad had been laid off from his job in Las Vegas. There he had worked for an aerospace company on a government contract running the air-combat training system at Nellis Air-force Base. He had been in that line of work since he left the Navy when I was six months old. We had a brief stop in Arkansas, where he was from, while my dad figured out what was next. He decided to change careers, as the stress of the defense industry was taking a toll on his health. He was hired to teach telecommunications at Northwest Mississippi Community College. So, we packed up our belongings and moved from Arkansas to Mississippi. This was a huge change for our family. Not only were we living in a new town and state, but my sister and I also began college. A new town and a new state also meant that we needed to find a new church. So, we started visiting churches and ended up joining Highland Baptist Church in Senatobia. It was there I met Dr. Clayton Cloer. Back then he was just Brother Clayton. Clayton was the pastor of Highland Baptist Church, and he would be the first person to teach me how to share my faith. I remember attending a class on soul winning. It was in this class that I received a three-ring binder with the title "The Soul Winner's Notebook." This book was basically a workbook put together by Clayton from the Personal Evangelism class he took in seminary under Dr. B. Gray Allison. I too would eventually take Personal Evangelism under Dr. Allison, but before that, the Soul Winner's Notebook would be my guide for how to share Jesus with lost people. Not only would I go through that notebook myself as a student, but I took it all around the world and used it to train people in how to share their faith. I am grateful for Clayton who taught me to share the Gospel.

I am also grateful for Dr. Allison who trained Clayton. And I am grateful for who-ever trained Dr. Allison – though I'm not sure who it was. It may have been Jesus personally, because Dr. Allison seemed that old to me as a sixteen-year-old boy.

As we begin this section on how to share the Gospel, I am still to this day indebted to "The Soul Winner's Notebook." While the plan of salvation that I am going to share for you is not the same as I learned from Clayton and Dr. Allison, it is heavenly influenced by them. Now that I have years of witnessing under my belt, as well as years of training other people how to witness, I have made tweaks to how I originally shared the Gospel as I continue to seek to improve my ability to share the Good News.

Tips for Witnessing

Here are some tips that will help guide you as you seek to share the good news with lost people.

1. Listen

Whenever I find myself witnessing to a lost person, I truly want them to be born again. Jesus has done such a wonderful work in my life that I don't want anyone to miss it. Also, I understand the dire consequences of rejecting Jesus – and I don't want anyone to experience the wrath that will come from such a decision. Know-ing this, I have at times found myself quick to speak, but slow to listen. Instead of hearing what the person has to say, I often find myself forming my response to their statements. People need to know that we are concerned about them. The best way you can demonstrate this is to truly listen to what they have to say. You don't have to agree, but you will earn the right to speak by hearing what they believe. Don't just act concerned about what they have to say, be concerned!

2. Don't expect a lost person to have the same standards you do.

I spent the first half of my ministry serving in the Bible Belt (the Southern part of the United States). I then moved to Las Vegas, where I have been pastoring for the last fourteen years. After living in and doing ministry in Vegas for a few years I realized a mistake that I, along with so many in the Bible Belt make, that is, I spent time trying to cut down fruit instead of dealing with root issues. I have seen Chris-tians, while trying to share their faith, get angry and even start yelling because someone did not believe what they believe or because a person used foul or blasphemous language. I've seen Christians get very upset because lost people do not hold the Word of God in high standing. **You cannot expect a lost person to act like a saved person!** Remember, do not get angry, but rather, realize that their eyes are closed to the things of God. Rebuking a person because of foul language, or because of ungodly behavior is trying to cut down fruit instead of dealing with the root issue – they don't know or love God. A person who simply addresses fruit instead of dealing with the root issue is only seeking behavior modification. A lost person doesn't need to stop cursing or live a more moral life. He or she needs to be radically saved by Jesus and transformed by the Gospel. Pray that the Lord would open their eyes and allow them to see. Also remember, that even if they may say they do not believe what you are saying is true, the reality is that the Holy Spirit is bearing testimony to your words, and He will draw them to the Father.

3. Find out what the person is trusting in for salvation.

Many people go to the doctor for regular checkups and find out that something major is wrong. The doctor finds the problem by doing diagnostic tests. He may do blood work, x-rays, or other tests. The point is, he finds the problem by doing a thorough examination. You can do a spiritual examination on a person by finding out what he is trusting in for salvation. Most people do not know that they are lost. Many believe that everything is just fine between them and God. Some are not sure if everything is fine, but their lives seem to be going OK, so there is no need to really examine where they stand with God. You can, by asking a simple question, find out what a person is trusting in for salvation and thereby diagnose his spiritual condition. Now, let me say that this is not judging whether someone is going to hell; it is finding out what a person is trusting in for salvation and comparing it with the Bible. If the two do not line up, then you need to inform the person of a major problem – according to the Bible, he is lost.

Here are two variations of a question that you can ask to find out what a person is trusting in:

   a. How does someone get to Heaven?

   b. What are the requirements to go to Heaven?

John 3:16 states: "For God so loved the world, that he gave his only Son, that whoever believes in him should not perish but have eternal life." That word "believe" in the original Greek means to trust. People who put their trust in Jesus as Lord and Savior will not perish but have eternal life. What the above questions seek to discover is what a person is trusting in for salvation. There are a number of things people trust in for salvation:

- **Being a good person** – Many people that I talk to believe they are good. This is called "Relative Righteousness." Compared to others, they are good. There are two problems with this position. First, it seems that a person always compares himself with someone who will make himself look good. Second, we are not to compare ourselves to other people, but rather to God's standard. If we compare ourselves to God's standard, we will see that we all fall short. This position also reveals that a person believes going to Heaven is based on a set of scales. If your good works outweigh your bad works, then you are going to Heaven. The problem, however, is that God does not operate on a scale. He has given us His law. Either we have obeyed it or broken it. An illustration I like to use is that if I get pulled over by a policeman for speeding, I cannot argue that most of the time I was going under the speed limit and therefore I should not get a ticket. It doesn't matter how much time you spend not breaking the law, if you break it once then you must face the consequences.

- **Religious affiliation** – Sometimes when I am talking to folks about salvation, they are quick to point to their religious affiliation as to why they should go to Heaven. I've had people tell me they are Catholic, or Baptist, or any number of religions. We do not get to Heaven simply by being part of any religious group.

- **Religious works / rituals** – It is not uncommon for people to trust in their religious works or having gone through various religious rituals in order to go to Heaven. When asked about what it takes to go to Heaven people will respond with: going to church, being baptized, or giving to the church. While these are all good things to do, they do not save a person.

- **Godly parents or grandparents** – Occasionally, I will have someone tell me how godly his parents or grandparents are. I remember asking someone about what he was trusting in to go to Heaven, and he began explaining how his father was a pastor. While it is a blessing to have godly parents and/or grandparents, their faith cannot save you.

- **The "Jesus Plus" Gospel** – While there are many false gospels in the world, the one that seems to be the most prevalent in areas with a Christian or Catholic majority is what I like to call the "Jesus Plus" gospel. This false gospel is where you mix a little bit of Jesus in with good works. When asking what someone is trusting in to get to Heaven, people will tell me about their good works, but then at the end of the witness tell me they have already been saved. Sometimes this is because they grew up in church hearing the Gospel, and intellectually believe in Jesus, but are not really trusting Him alone for salvation. I grew up going to church and I believed what I had been taught about Jesus, but I still was trusting in good works and religion to get me to Heaven. It wasn't until I realized that there is nothing I can do to get myself to Heaven that I truly put my trust in Jesus alone for salvation. There is a difference in intellectually believing that Jesus died for sinners and coming to the place that you realize you are lost and the ONLY way to be saved is to call upon Jesus as Lord. It is not a combination of your "righteous" works and the work of Jesus on the cross. As Ephesians 2:8-9 teaches, it is by grace through faith that we are saved, not through works.

If the person answers the questions with any other answer than trusting in Jesus as Lord and Savior, then there is a problem. You are not condemning him to Hell, but you are saying that based on what he told you, the Bible teaches that he is lost. *Be sure to repeat a person's answer to him to ensure that you understood what he said and meant.*

4. Sometimes you need to ask for permission to share.

When I was first trained in evangelism, I was taught to always ask permission to share what the Bible says about going to Heaven. Sometimes when you share the Gospel with people, they become defensive and will tell you that they will not be pushed into anything. By asking permission, you can remind them that they told you it would be all right for you to show them what the Bible says. With that said, my training was geared more for sharing the Gospel with strangers than with people that I know personally. When sharing with a stranger, I often will ask permission to share the Word of God. I do not, however, usually ask people that I know or that I am engaged with in a meaningful conversation. I typically only ask permission in "drive-by" witnessing encounters.

5. Give the person an opportunity to receive Jesus.

Sales experts will tell you that one of the biggest challenges in training people in the art of selling is getting a person to "make the ask." It is easy for many people to talk about a product, but it is difficult for them to close the deal by asking if the person is ready to buy. Some people believe that you should only present the Gospel, but not give an invitation. To put it in selling terms, you should never "make the ask." Scripture, however, gives clear examples and teaching that we should invite people to be saved. Acts 16:31 "And they said, 'Believe in the Lord Jesus, and you will be saved, you and your house.'" Here Paul and Silas give the Philippian jailer an opportunity to receive Jesus – and he did! We should never be embarrassed to give people the opportunity to receive Jesus. Just giving them a head knowledge of the Gospel alone will not help them; they must receive it.

2 Corinthians 5:20 "Therefore, we are ambassadors for Christ, as though God were making an appeal through us; we beg you on behalf of Christ, be reconciled to God."

6. Closing a witness

If the person comes to trust Jesus as his Lord and Savior, then you need to share with him that he needs to make his decision public, be baptized, and join a local church. Get his name and contact information so that you can make sure follow-up is done. Also, confirm that he has access to a Bible and encourage him to begin reading it. The Gospel of John is a great place for a new believer to begin reading.

If the person does not receive Christ, ask him this question, "Let's say that later tonight you decide you want to receive Jesus as your Lord and Savior, how do you go about doing that?" The reason for this question is to ensure that he understands exactly how to receive Jesus. If he doesn't know, go over how to receive Jesus with him. If he still does not want to be saved, ask him if you can pray for him before you leave. Pray and ask God to open his eyes and work in his life and draw him unto Himself. Thank the person for listening and get any contact information you can. Give him a way to get in touch with you in case he wants to talk to you later. Also, leave a track or a Bible with him if you can.

7. Remember that the Gospel is good news!

While I am always grateful to see people witnessing, I am not always in agreement in how they go about doing so. Living in Vegas I see many Christians who like to go down to the Las Vegas Strip and do street evangelism / preaching. I have found myself at times listening to some of these people and have asked myself the question: "I wonder if they realize that the word Gospel means good news?" It is true that before we get to the good news we must deal with bad news – the fact that we are all sinners, and we are guilty before a holy God. Our presentation of the Gospel should be done with great joy and compassion. Jesus spent his ministry talking to lost people about the Kingdom of God. Jesus was not soft on sin, yet he conducted himself in such a way that lost people were drawn to hear what He had to say. Many walked always lost, but that is because they rejected the message, not the presentation. I believe the biblical model for witnessing is to do it in a way that is with great joy as we announce good news. As my mentor, Dr. Clayton Cloer taught me, we should have the same excitement as if we were giving away a million dollars. If someone rejects Jesus, I want it to be because they reject the message, not the way the message was delivered.

8. Don't be afraid to say: "I don't know, but I'll research that."

I have often had Christians express fear that they may be asked a question of which they do not know the answer. First, by sharing your faith with someone you are not claiming to be an expert in theology or the Bible. You are sharing about what Jesus did for you and what the Bible teaches about salvation. Second, I have found that people respect when you say: "I don't know, but I will research that." It is better to answer honestly that you do not know the answer to their question than to try and fake an answer. Also, no matter how much training you do, most likely you will come across questions that you cannot answer. I have a Ph.D. from seminary, but people still sometimes ask me questions that I cannot answer on the spot. I do, however, try to be faithful to research their questions and get back to them with an answer. We often see in the Bible where people came to faith and immediately started sharing with other lost people. They didn't wait until they had formal theological training to start witnessing – they just started witnessing. A great example of this is in John 4. Jesus speaks to a Samaritan woman at a well and she believes. She then goes and shares with her entire village and many of them believed.

Personal Testimony

One of the most powerful ways a believer can witness is to share his or her testimony. Jesus said, "you shall be my witnesses." A witness is someone who gives a verbal first-hand account of something he has seen or heard. Before I was a Christian, I could not be a witness because everything I knew about God was second hand. However, the moment I got saved I became a witness for I had experienced first-hand what God could do in my life. Too few people know how to share their testimony in a manner that can be used of God to win someone to Jesus.

The goal of this section is help you develop what I call your "canned testimony." I use the word canned because I think of a can of soup. Soup companies work hard to ensure that every can of soup they produce tastes the same. I want you to have a basic presentation of your testimony that is exactly the same every time you share it. That way you can confidently share it almost without even thinking about it. This is important because sometimes when you witness to people you find yourself getting nervous. Having a "canned" testimony helps you overcome this.

Another reason I like the term canned testimony is because just like with a can of soup, you can add to it and customize it. Once you are comfortable sharing your canned testimony, you can customize it if needed to help you connect with the individual you're speaking with. Maybe you have a similar experience with the person you are witnessing to that you want to include in your testimony because you think it will help you connect with him on a deeper level. It is easy to add such stories when you are comfortable sharing your testimony.

Let me give you a few tips in sharing your testimony:

1. Follow the five "B's" of sharing – **"Be brief brother, be brief!"** You should be able to share your testimony in **three to five minutes**. Now, you may have times where you build on this for a longer witness, but it is good to have a basic, simple presentation of what Jesus has done in your life.

2. Be organized in how you present your thoughts. Your testimony should be broken down into three parts:

   a. **Before you were saved** – what were your trusting in for salvation. Did you believe in God? Give a clear picture of what your life was like.

   b. **When did you get saved** – where were you, what was happening to bring you to the point of decision? How did you get saved?

   c. **What is your life like now that you are saved** – how have you grown? What difference is there in your life? How has God changed your life?

3. Look for a theme. For some people, their underlying theme is peace. Years ago, there was a senior adult lady in the church I attended named Beth Baker. Beth grew up in church, but she never had peace that she was going to Heaven when she died. She thought she could get peace by being more zealous. So, she served in just about every capacity that she could at the church. She worked with the children, she sang in the choir, she helped with the hospitality team. She even went on mission trips. The problem, however, is that even though she became very zealous and faithful in serving, she still did not have peace. She would lie awake at night scared that if she died, she would wake up in Hell. One Sunday our pastor was preaching on peace. Though this happened almost thirty years ago, I still remember it like it was yesterday. Our pastor was teaching that if you never have peace, it may be because you have never had authentic salvation. When the invitation time came, tears were coming down Beth's face as the choir robe came off and she went down and

accepted Jesus as Lord and Savior. After that day she had peace. I remember standing beside Beth's hospital bed several years later as she was dying from cancer. I asked her if she still had peace. Her face lit up and she told me that she had a peace that surpasses all understanding.

While Beth's theme was peace, for others, their theme is good works. Before they were saved, they were trusting in their own good works to get them in Heaven. Now that they are saved, they have put their trust in Jesus' work on the cross. A theme gives people something to identify with even if their theme is not the same as yours. It is like a handle on a cup – it makes it easier to grasp.

4. Practice your testimony. It is important to practice sharing your testimony. You want people to give you feedback on whether it is clear and understandable to a lost person. Sometimes people insert language that unchurched people will not know. For example, sometimes people will say that they were at a revival when they got saved. Unchurched people may not know what a revival is. Instead, say that you were at a special service at your church. Having other believers help you polish your testimony Is very important.

When I'm training people to share their testimonies, I have them practice with the group and/or with me. Each time they share they are given feedback on what worked and what could be improved until it is really polished. I then give them an assignment to share it with someone "safe." A safe person is someone who they know is already a believer. After they have done this a few times and received feedback, I ask them to share it with an "unsafe" person. This is a person that as far as they know is not a believer. I also give them a helpful way to start the conversation. I tell them to ask the person if they can help them with an assignment from a class they are taking. They need to share their testimony with someone and ask that person to give them feedback. The beauty of this method is that it not only gives you the opportunity to share your testimony, but it requires that you discuss it. You need their feedback. Also, people LOVE to give their opinion (feedback). I have found this an effective way to start the conversation.

5. Write out your testimony. Some people do not want to take the time to write out their testimony. By not writing it down, it hinders the process of polishing it. Remember, that you are trying to develop your "canned testimony." This means that it should be almost the same word for word each time you share it. Writing it down helps you achieve this. So, take the time and write it down. A good rule of thumb is that it should take up one page. Remember, to divide it into the three sections – Before I was saved, when I got saved, and my life after I got saved.

As an example of a concise testimony, let me share with you my personal testimony:

I grew up going to church. It seemed like every time the doors were opened at the church, the Creecy family was there. I was active in Sunday school, children's choir, plus I was best friends with the pastor's son. I was pretty much a "good" kid. I did well in school and for the most part, I did what my parents told me. I had even been baptized. I thought that the way to Heaven was through good works, and that I was probably well on my way. I figured that if you had to be good to get into Heaven, then I was most likely going to make it there.

When I was ten years old, my family and I moved to Beaufort, South Carolina. There I began to attend a private Christian school. It was at this school that I first started hearing the Gospel. I had heard of Jesus, and I knew that he had died on a cross, but I did not understand that He died to take my place. I did not know that even though I thought I was a "good" kid, that I was a sinner and that my sin deserves death. After several weeks of hearing the Gospel, I knew that I was lost. I knew that I was trusting in my own good works to get me to Heaven, but that my works would not meet God's standard. One day, while in my home, I prayed to receive Jesus as my Lord and Savior. I knew that my parents and my sister were not Christians, but I knew I had to make a decision to follow Jesus. It was not long after I got saved, that my parents and sister also came to know Jesus as their Lord and Savior. We were all baptized together in the Beaufort River.

Since becoming a Christian, I still seek to do good. The difference now is that I am not trusting in my own deeds to get me to Heaven, I am trusting Jesus' work on the cross. He saved me from my sin and brought me from a religion into a relationship with Him – the Living God. Now I go to church, not to fulfill a required activity, but because I love to gather with believers and worship the God who paid so much in order for me to be saved!

Your Testimony

Before I was saved....

When I got saved....

My life after I got saved…

One Final Word About Your Testimony

Before we wrap up this section on sharing your personal testimony, I need to address a question that I am often asked: "What if I don't know when I was saved?" I have encountered quite a few people over the years that really struggled with sharing their testimonies because they are not sure about when they were saved. This confusion is because of one of two things. One, a person has never been saved. Or two, they have been saved, but they are not sure of the exact moment. Many times, while teaching this subject in seminars, I have seen people realize that they are lost and decide right there in the meeting to give their lives to Jesus. I do believe that churches, even Gospel preaching churches, have many people who come week in and week out but are still lost. Because of this, they do not have a testimony.

The second reason why someone might have this question is because even though they are saved, they are not sure of the exact time and place they were saved. For some people, they had a season where they were introduced to the Gospel, and sometime during that season they believed. One person once described it like crossing a border in the woods at night. The next day you realize you crossed the border the previous night, but you're not exactly sure when. Now, some people would say that if you don't know the exact moment you were saved then you are not saved. I'm not sure I believe that. I have talked to people that I genuinely believe are saved, but they aren't sure of the exact moment they believed on Jesus. When someone tells me they are not sure of when they were saved, I ask them the following questions:

- Do you believe Jesus died for your sins and was raised on the third day?

- Do you trust in Jesus alone for your salvation?

- Do you confess that Jesus is Lord?

If the person believes in all of these, then I try to figure out what period in his life did he learn about and believe in these truths? For some, it was over a period of time attending a Bible study that they understood and believed the Gospel. Their testimony may sound something like: "I started attending a Bible study on Tuesday nights. It was during this Bible study that I realized Jesus died for my sins and that He is the only way to Heaven. It was during this time that I believed in Jesus as my Lord and Savior.

Some people have told me that they have always believed. These are people who were raised in church. The problem is that you are not born a Christian. There has to be a time where you move from just knowing and believing the Bible stories you were taught as a kid, to realizing that you need saving. At what point did your faith really become yours?

Chapter 3
Using the Bible to Share Your Faith

Basic Plan for Sharing Your Faith

Years ago, I had a group of college guys that I spent two years discipling. We would meet once a week for two hours. The first hour we discussed whatever they wanted to talk about. Sometimes we spent that hour talking about spiritual things, sometimes we talked about life and ministry, sometimes we talked about sports. Whatever they wanted to discuss was fair game during that hour. The second hour we discussed what I had prepared for them. One of the first things I taught them was how to witness. I remember after we had spent a few weeks training, I took them out on campus to practice witnessing. We walked through the campus and approached people and asked them if we could talk to them for a minute. We would then begin to share the Gospel. When we finished, we had a time of debriefing. I asked my disciples what surprised them the most about what they experienced. Their response was that they could not believe how many people had not heard the Gospel. We were in the Bible Belt – hadn't everyone heard the Gospel? If so many people in the Bible Belt had not heard the Gospel, then how much more so in other places in the United States?

As sad as it is that so many people have not heard the Gospel, what bothers me even more is that I have found in almost thirty years of ministry, that many Christians, even folks who have been Christians for decades, struggle with being able to take the Bible and clearly walk someone through the Gospel. Unfortunately, this is an indictment against our churches. We must do better to ensure that every Christian can share the Gospel.

While sharing your testimony is a powerful way to share the Gospel, every Christian should be able to take the Word of God and witness to a lost person. This sounds intimidating to some, but it is not very difficult at all. The beautiful thing about the approach I am going to share with you is that you are simply having the person read the passages and then giving him a little explanation. The Word does all the heavy lifting.

Some Tips Before You Start

1. It is important to memorize the passages in this section. Memorizing them will give you a greater command of the verses. Plus, in the event that you are not able to have someone actually read the verses, you are still able to use the Word of God to witness.

2. Always try to show the person the scripture as you read it. This reinforces that you are sharing from the Bible. Now, I use to teach, as I was once taught, that every believer should carry a pocket New Testament with him everywhere he went. For years I always had a pocket New Testament in my back pocket just in case I had an opportunity to share the Gospel. I always called it the "Compressed Version" because I sat on it every day. It didn't take long before it looked to be in sad shape. I no longer carry a pocket New Testament with me everywhere I go because I now have a smart phone with multiple Bible apps. There are many free Bible apps available that you can utilize for witnessing.

3. Read the verse to the person while showing him the screen but avoid asking the person to read the verse out loud. Asking someone to read the passage out loud can create an awkward situation if the person is afraid of reading in front of another person or is unable to read at all.

4. Practice enough so that you are comfortable walking through the plan of salvation. The more times you practice, the more comfortable you will be when you actually begin sharing with someone.

Part 1 – The Bad News

1. What is the person trusting in for salvation?

The first step in witnessing is to determine whether you need to witness to the person. This is done by finding out what a person is trusting in for salvation. Some may ask, "Is this judging?" The answer is no. We cannot read a person's heart and declare for certain that he or she is saved. We can, however, ask a person what he or she is trusting in and compare it to the Word of God.

Ask: "What are the requirements for going to Heaven?"

Whatever a person believes are the requirements to go to Heaven shows what he is trusting in to get there.

2. Get permission to share what the Bible says.

If a person gives any answer other than salvation in Jesus Christ alone, then proceed with the witnesses. Understand that a lot of people will most likely give you a works-based answer. A works-based answer is any answer that points to being good or religious. Some will even give you a "Jesus plus" answer. This is where they are trusting in Jesus plus good works. Any Gospel that is not Jesus alone is a false Gospel.

The reason you want to ask for permission is because you are about to engage in spiritual warfare. No matter how sweetly you present the Gospel it can be offensive. Asking permission demonstrates that you are not forcing your beliefs on anyone, but rather, as a concerned person, you desire to share truth. Also, if a person does get angry, you can gently remind him or her that you do not want to force anything, and that you asked permission.

Ask: "May I quickly show you on my phone's Bible app what the Bible says about going to Heaven?"

The Need for Salvation

You want to demonstrate three truths through your witness. First, you want the person to see the need for salvation. Second, you want the person to see that salvation has been provided. Third, you want the person to see how to receive salvation.

As you move forward you should simply read the passage and then briefly explain it.

- **Romans 3:10 – [10] as it is written: "None is righteous, no, not one;**

This verse simply says that there are none who are perfect. We have all made mistakes. We have all done wrong things. Have you ever known anyone who is perfect? It is important to state that you have made mistakes and done wrong things and ask the person is he has also made mistakes and done wrong things.

- **Romans 3:23 – [23] for all have sinned and fall short of the glory of God,**

Again, this verse says that we ALL have sinned and fallen short of God's standard. Sin is breaking God's law. A great question to ask is: "Do you agree that everyone sins – or does wrong things?"

If his answer is yes, then ask him, "Do you believe that you and I are both sinners?" If he is not sure, remind him that the verse you just read says that ALL people are sinners.

You can also use the Ten Commandments to help people see that they are sinners. You can ask, "Have you ever told a lie?" "Have you ever disobeyed your parents?" By doing these things a person breaks God's law. Breaking God's law makes you a sinner.

- **Romans 6:23a – "For the wages of sin is death…"**

A wage is something earned. Imagine you worked all week, and it was payday and your boss said, "I don't feel like paying you." Would you be mad? Of course you would – you earned that pay.

When we sin, we earn death – not just physical death, but also spiritual death. Spiritual death is separation from God. If we die, being spiritually dead, then we will face eternity separated from God in a very real place called Hell. Because of our sins, we deserve to be punished.

What is important to point out about the above verses is that it shows that we have all broken God's law. Most people believe that the entrance to Heaven is based on two scales. In one scale, all your bad works are placed. In the other, all your good works. If the bad outweighs the good, then you go to the bad place. If your good outweighs the bad, then you go to Heaven. The problem is that God does not use a scale, but rather, He judges based on whether or not you have broken His law.

When someone breaks the law, he must receive the punishment for doing so. Imagine if you were pulled over by a police officer for speeding. The officer walks up to the side of your car and says, "You were going 50mph in a 35mph zone." In response, you tell the officer that before he clocked your speed, you had been going 15mph under the speed limit for most of the time you had been driving. You argue that your time under the speed limit outweighs the time you spent over the speed limit, and he should therefore not give you a ticket. Or let's say that you murdered someone. In court you argue that while you did murder someone, you have only done it once. Therefore, if you look at the days of your life that you didn't murder someone, they far outweigh the one single day that you did commit murder. In both situations, you would still be found guilty. Why? **Because it doesn't matter how often or how long you have obeyed the law, it only matters to the court if you have broken the law.** Both illustrations seem ludicrous. Yet this is the same type of argument people try to make with God.

The bad news is that we have all broken God's law and stand guilty before Him. Furthermore, the mandatory sentence for breaking God's law is death, which means eternal separation from Him in a very real place called Hell.

At this point I want to pivot the conversation. I usually say something like this: "While this is really bad news, I am not here to share bad news, but rather, good news. God has provided someone who has taken our punishment for our sin."

The Provision of Salvation

- **John 3:16 – [16] "For God so loved the world, that he gave his only Son, that whoever believes in him should not perish but have eternal life.**

Even though we have sinned against God, He still loves us. He demonstrated His love for us by sending His only son, Jesus, to die on the cross for our sins. Jesus was willing to take our punishment for us so that we would not have to. Whoever believes in Jesus will not perish but will have everlasting life.

Some people believe that because God is a god of love that He will not punish sin. If God did not punish sin, then He would not be just. Imagine that you had a family member brutally murdered. The criminal who killed your loved one was caught and found guilty of the crime beyond all reasonable doubt. The day finally comes where the judge is going to pronounce the sentence. Just think about how you would feel if the judge said that he was a judge of love and that he therefore would not punish the murderer. Would you think that judge was really acting in love. Did that judge provide justice? You would be angry, and rightfully so.

God must punish sin, but because He does love us, He sent Jesus to die for our sins. The just for the unjust. He took our punishment and offers us salvation if we will simply believe in Him.

What does it mean to believe in Jesus? It means to trust in Him. To trust in Jesus, you must stop trusting in whatever you have been trusting in for salvation. I used to trust in being religious and doing good works. I had to forsake my trust in those things and put my trust that Jesus paid for my sins and is my only hope for salvation.

- **Romans 6:23b - . . . but the free gift of God is eternal life in Christ Jesus our Lord.**

Jesus is the greatest gift that the world has ever known. Jesus took the punishment for our sins, and He now offers us the free gift of salvation.

When does a gift become yours? It is not when it is offered. A gift can be offered yet refused. A gift does not become yours until you receive it. What is important to emphasize here is that **salvation is not a reward to be earned, but rather, a gift to be received.** If something must be earned or purchased, it is not a gift. Most people are trying to earn their way to Heaven by being a good person. This makes Heaven a reward. The problem is that Heaven cannot be earned because we have all broken God's law. The good news, however, is that God offers us the gift of salvation. The question now becomes, "How do I receive this gift?"

Receiving Salvation

- **Romans 10:9 – [9] because, if you confess with your mouth that Jesus is Lord and believe in your heart that God raised him from the dead, you will be saved.**

This verse again shows how to be saved. We confess Jesus as Lord, we believe that God raised him from the dead, and we are saved.

- **Romans 10:13 – [13] For "everyone who calls on the name of the Lord will be saved."**

Now that we see that God offers the free gift of salvation through Jesus Christ, I want to share with you how to receive that gift.

This verse says that whoever calls upon the name of the Lord will be saved. Let's look at a few words here.

Whoever – that means salvation is open to all. It does not matter where you've been, what you've done – Jesus is willing and wanting to save you!

Calls – this word means to cry out. It is a picture of someone who is drowning, calling out for help. In order to cry out for help, you must realize that you need help. You must confess to Jesus that you are a sinner and ask him to forgive you of your sins and to save you.

Lord – when you call out, you call out to the Lord Jesus. The word Lord means boss. By calling out to the Lord you are recognizing Jesus as the boss of your life. You are now surrendering to His Lordship over you.

Will be saved – when you put your trust in Jesus' work on the cross, then you can know for certain that you are saved! Salvation is not based on our work, but on Jesus' work- therefore we can know for certain that we are saved!"

- **Ask the person if he would like to receive Jesus as his Lord and Savior?**

If the person says yes, then say:

"Right here you can pray and asks Jesus to forgive you of your sins, be the boss of your life, and save you. By receiving Jesus as Lord, you will be saved."

Here is a model prayer:

"Lord Jesus, I admit that I am a sinner. I believe that you came and died on the cross for my sins and rose from the grave and I ask you to forgive me and to save me. I also invite you to be the Lord of my life. Save me Lord Jesus. Thank you for saving me, help me to never be ashamed of you."

Closing

If the person received Jesus, then share with him that he needs to get involved in a local church. Be sure to get his information or at least give him information about a good local Bible believing, Bible teaching church.

I wish every person I witnessed to would say yes to Jesus, but that has not been the case. Many times, people are not ready to trust Jesus as Lord and Savior. When someone does not get saved, I want to do two things.

1. I want to ask what is keeping him from accepting Jesus. Sometimes a person tells me that he needs to get some things straight in his life before he gets saved. In that case, I remind him that he is trying to earn the gift instead of receiving it. Sometimes a person just doesn't believe. By asking why a person isn't ready can help you answer objections a person might have.

2. If the person did not receive Jesus, then I want to make sure he understands how to be saved. I usually ask him: "If tonight you wanted to receive Jesus as your Lord and Savior, would you please tell me how to do it?" How a person answers this question will help you know if he understood the gospel. It will also give you an opportunity to clarify the Gospel. The goal with this question, is to know that the person understands how to be saved. The Holy Spirit will continue to bear testimony to what you have shared, and this person will know how to respond.

In this section I have expanded on the verses in greater detail than you might in an actual witnessing encounter. I am including a more streamlined script to help you in Appendix C. Memorizing the script will help you be more confident as you begin to share the Gospel.

Chapter 4
Missional Living

A few years ago, I had a conversation with a gentleman I met in a cigar lounge. He was a successful businessman who had made a good living. He was very sharp, had a deep love for Jesus, and was generous with what God had blessed him with financially. As we were discussing different things about our faith in Jesus, he expressed to me a great desire he had. He wanted to get out of the business world and start a non-profit organization that would impact the Kingdom of God. He lamented about how he was tired of going to work every day to spend his life toiling for things that did not matter for eternity. I so appreciated his honesty. So many people would want his life. A successful businessman with a good family and a large income. For this man, however, that wasn't his heart's desire. He wanted to have more Kingdom impact. I asked him a question: "Do you see your workplace as a mission field?" He looked a little shocked. He responded that he had never really thought of it that way. I then asked him how he thought he would feel about his workplace if he took time every day before he walked into his office to pray and ask God to give him Kingdom impact amongst everyone he interacted with that day. Did he think that may change his view from toiling all day for things that don't matter for eternity, or would it bring new life into his work experience as he saw it as his mission field? Again, he stated that he had never thought about it that way and that he would start doing it.

The problem with that gentleman is not that he didn't have a mission field, but rather, he didn't recognize that he was in the middle of a mission field. It reminds me of John 4:35 – " Do you not say, 'There are yet four months, then comes the harvest'? Look, I tell you, lift up your eyes, and see that the fields are white for harvest." Here Jesus challenged the disciples to see the harvest. So often we think the harvest is somewhere else, when in reality, the harvest is all around us. Too often we think we need to be in a different field when we are in a field that is just waiting to be harvested. We don't see that God has placed us where we are and has given us relationships that He wants to use to grow His Kingdom.

As a pastor, I have learned that I am sometimes limited in the circles that I have access to. I have church members who, because of what they do for a living, have access to circles of people that I would have a hard time reaching. Some of them live in gated communities that we can't access for door-to-door witnessing. Some of them have access to people of great influence that I would never encounter. Some of them hangout in places that I could never afford. Plus, my church members naturally have many more meaningful relationships with lost people than I as a pastor will ever have. All the people I work with at the office are saved. I work at a church. I sometimes envy church members who get to enter a mission field every day for hours at a time. The problem is that many Christians do not see the mission field where they have been placed by God.

In my early days of witnessing, most opportunities were centered around what I like to call "drive-by" witnessing encounters. They included going to malls, parks, street corners, college campuses, and walking up to strangers and sharing the Gospel. I also did church visitation. Most of those visits were with total strangers. Now let me clearly say that I am for drive-by witnessing. There is a great need for widespread seed sowing of the Gospel. It is also a Biblical model of evangelism. Believers like the Apostle Paul would go to new cities and just find strangers to share the Gospel. With that said, I also understand that walking up to a total stranger and engaging them in any conversation, much less a spiritual conversation, is extremely scary for most people. While some people love it and thrive off that type of witnessing experience, many others tremble at the idea.

While drive-by witnessing is a Biblical model for witnessing, it is not the only Biblical model. What we clearly see in the New Testament is that the Gospel flowed through relationships. While people like the Apostle Paul shared the Gospel with total strangers, a lot of the believers witnessed to the people around them. This is demonstrated in the first evangelist we see in the Gospels. In John 4, the Bible records an encounter Jesus had with a Samaritan woman at a well. She had an encounter with Jesus and immediately went to her village, where she would have probably known everyone, and started telling them about Jesus. The result was that many in her village became believers because of her testimony. Furthermore, throughout the book of Acts, there are multiple examples that when people were saved, they immediately gathered their households to hear the Gospel.

We need more drive-by witnessing. But what we also desperately need, are more people to engage in missional living. This is a term that has been used a lot in evangelism and church planting books, but what does it mean? Let me take some time to unpack it for you.

Definition

In Christianity, missional living is the adoption of the posture, thinking, behaviors, and practices of a missionary to engage others with the gospel message.

Important Concepts

- **All Christians are Missionaries**

We must repent of the idea that only some are called to be missionaries. While we may not all be called to move permanently overseas to reach another culture, we have all been called to be witnesses for Jesus Christ. We must, therefore, begin to live as a missionary.

A problem with challenging people to live as missionaries, is that most people do not understand what missionaries do. They think that means they need to start an orphanage, or hospital, or begin preaching on street corners. The reality is that most missionaries in the world do not operate this way. As the focus of missions has turned more and more to unreached areas, the activity of missionaries has drastically changed over the years. Missionaries serving in restricted countries cannot enter as missionaries. They have to find other ways to get into the country. Many of them get jobs or start businesses to obtain the visas required to live in the country. They can't go on street corners and preach, or they will be arrested or killed. They must live amongst the people, build relationships, and share the Gospel. These missionaries are constantly looking for opportunities to connect with lost people to share the Gospel. They target the people they work with, their neighbors, and the friends they make. They look for ways and places people connect. You can find the missionaries hanging out at tea shops, joining soccer clubs, attending cultural events. Everywhere missionaries go they are on the hunt for people with whom they can share the Gospel. This is the mindset we need in the church.

Missionaries work hard to embed themselves in their target cultures. They recognize that when they arrive in a new culture that they are outsiders. Through language and cultural acquisition, which can be exhausting, they slowly become more and more accepted in the culture. I think one of the challenges in the Western church is that we do not realize that we have become such a distinct sub-culture that we are no longer connected to our target culture. I think this is best seen in the fact that the longer someone is a believer, the more detached he is from lostness. More and more they find that all their time is taken up with fellow Christians. I also see the disconnect when I train Christians in how to share their testimonies. Since becoming saved, they have taken on a new language full of words that an unchurched person does not know. I have to help them remove the churchese language so that their testimony will clearly communicate.

We do have to be careful that in trying to connect with our target culture that we do not embrace unbiblical practices or thinking. We must stay grounded in the Word and live in Christian fellowship, lest we stray from the right path. We should, however, as missionaries try to connect with our target culture, seek to connect with our community, which is our target culture.

- **Outward Focused**

We have replaced the Great Commission of "go ye" with "come y'all." Missionaries do not wait for lost people to come to them, but rather, they go to the lost people. We have lost this mindset in the North American church. Our churches need to make decisions that are outward focused. One of the most effective things some churches could do is streamline the number of activities they offer. I have known some church members that attend activities at the church four to five days a week. They spend so much time on the church campus that they do not have any time to invest in the lives of lost people. Church leaders need to constantly ask the question: "Is how we are doing church life getting people into the community?" Most churches, I'm afraid, are more concerned about how many people they get on their campuses each week as opposed to how many they are sending out into the harvest field.

- **Think Differently**

We must stop thinking in terms of "secular" and "sacred." The majority of people in our churches work in what we call "secular" jobs. The problem with this thinking is that we miss the fact that all of us are ministers of the Gospel. Our company may be "secular" in orientation, but if you are a Christian, you have been called to a "sacred" task. You have been called to be a missionary where you live, work, and play. Just like the gentleman I told you about at the opening of this chapter, you too should see your work as a sacred calling. You should see it as your mission field and ask God to give you influence in people's lives for the Gospel.

- ### Intentional Living

The key to Missional Living is intentional living. It is all about understanding who you are in Christ, what your calling is, and being focused on fulfilling that calling everywhere you go. It is not about creating more programs at the church under the name of evangelism, but rather, being intentional about winning people to Jesus Christ in every venue of your life. While I hope this book equips you to know how to share the Gospel, and that it gives you strategies on how to begin engaging your community, my greatest prayer for this book is that it will open your eyes to what God has called you to be and do and that you will live with greater intentionality than you ever have. Two major stumbling blocks to having the impact God desires you to have are apathy and distraction. Many of us, if we were honest, do not really care that so many people around us are going to die and go to Hell. It is like we have become immune to the reality that Hell is real, and many of the people we interact with everyday are going to end up in that horrible place. We also live busy lives. We want to invest in lost people, but we never get around to it. We are distracted by work, children, activities, and yes, church. We desire to have an impact, but we blink, and another year has gone by, and we still haven't witnessed. Learning to live intentionally is key to being an effective witness.

As previously mentioned, Jesus used the illustration of a harvest. When I moved to Arkansas as a teenager I learned a lot about harvesting. We moved from a brand-new house in Las Vegas to an old farmhouse in the middle of a cotton field in Arkansas. My dad was transitioning careers and spent a season working for one of his friends who was a cotton farmer. We arrived right as the harvest was beginning. During that time, I learned two important lessons about the harvest. One, the harvest is a race against time and elements. For those who are not familiar with cotton, it grows on a shrub. The shrub has bowls that open, and the cotton is inside the bowls. At the beginning of harvest season, the bowls begin to open and the farmers spray defoliant on the plants. The defoliant helps to open the bowls and dry out the cotton to make it easier to harvest. Once the bowls start to open, and the cotton is exposed to the elements, the clock is ticking. Every day that the cotton is exposed impacts the quality of the cotton. The farmers must hustle to get the cotton harvested before the quality becomes so low that it isn't worth picking. Farmers start early in the morning and work late into the night trying to gather their harvest. This same principle is true for most agricultural products. Once the produce is ripe, you must get it before is spoils.

The second lesson I learned about the harvest is that you must be intentional about getting the harvest. Farmers can't simply sit on the front porch and drink coffee and expect the harvest to be gathered. They become extremely intentional and set aside all distractions during the harvest season, least the harvest spoil in the field. Back before mechanized cotton harvesting, my dad grew up picking cotton. In those days, local schools stopped having classes until the harvest was complete. Everyone was needed in the fields.

As we think about the metaphor of harvest in the context of evangelism, the same two truths I learned in Arkansas apply to the harvest of souls. The clock is ticking. Every day people die and go to Hell. We think we have all the time in the world, but we don't. Second, if we are not intentional about the harvest of souls, then we will not bring in the harvest. There is so much that can distract us from the harvest, but we need to be like the farmer who sets aside all distractions to bring in the harvest.

The Three Domains of Life

Now that we understand that we should practice missional living, the question becomes: "Where do we start?" We are now going to transition to developing strategies for missional living. To approach this subject, we first need to understand that we spend most of our lives operating in three different domains. It is in these domains that we should begin to implement strategies that allow us to reach people with the Gospel. These three domains are known as first space, second space, and third space. First space is where you live. Second space is where you work (or go to school). Third space is where you spend your time in between first and second space.

Third space is the hardest domain for people to grasp, because it can look very different between one person and the next. We know what where we live means. We also know what where we work means. But where we spend our time in-between varies greatly. So, your third space could be church, sports teams for you or your children, bars, cigar lounges, organizations where you volunteer, or any other place that you willingly spend your time when you're not at home or work. The reason I say willingly is because we often spend some of our time in places that we wouldn't pick for fun but are necessary. Such places are the grocery store (though some people do love to go to the grocery store), doctor's office, or any other errand that must be done as part of our lives.

It is important to note that these three domains are not islands unto themselves - they often overlap. For example, you may spend a lot of time at the ball field watching your kid play baseball. In that environment, you become friends with some of his teammates' families. You invite them over for a BBQ on a Saturday afternoon. You have just overlapped your first and third spaces. Understanding that the domains overlap will be important as we begin developing evangelism strategies for these different domains.

Connecting with Lost People for a Purpose

The purpose of this section and the next is to help you do two things. First, in this section, I will help you learn to connect with groups of lost people. I've had multiple church members throughout the years tell me that they really don't know any lost people. That means the only form of evangelism available to them is drive-by witnessing. The reason Christians do not have meaningful relationships with lost people is because all their fellowship needs are met at the church and/or their families. The longer they are followers of Jesus, the more they find themselves disconnected from lost people. On one hand, this means that the church is doing fellowship well. On the other hand, it means that they are having little to no impact for the Kingdom. How do you balance having deep, meaningful relationships with your fellow Christians, while maintaining enough time to invest in the lives of lost people? The best place to turn for the answer is Jesus. He had deep relationships with His disciples. For the better part of three years, they lived together, ate together, traveled together, and served together. Yet, while Jesus established deep relationships with His disciples, He was still intentional about investing in the lives of lost people. When reading the Gospels, we often find Jesus meeting with and eating with lost people. He was intentional not to allow all of His time to be consumed by His disciples, but He was intentional to leave time for lost people.

For some Christians, to become effective in building relationships with lost people in their communities, they are going to have to step back from being so involved at church. That may mean they cannot go to every Bible study and event that the church offers. I believe the Biblical mandate for church involvement is that a believer should be a part of corporate worship, they should be actively involved in a small group of believers that shares life and grows in their walks with Jesus, and they should have some ministry that gets them involved with lost people in order to share the Gospel. This is very different than the Sunday morning service, Sunday night service, Sunday school, Discipleship training hour, and Wednesday night service or Bible Study. That alone is five hours a week at the church campus. The list doesn't include other roles that one might have at the church including serving on a committee or other Bibles studies that are offered at different times during the week. By spending that much time on the church campus, when does someone have time to invest in lost people?

Once you realize that you have to get off the church campus, you may be wondering how to connect with lost people in your community. I like to use the metaphor of a fishing hole. Connecting with groups of lost people is likened to finding a good fishing hole. Once you find the fishing hole, the question becomes how to effectively fish. How do you move the relationships from causal to deeper? How do you move conversations to the Gospel? How do you look for people who have interest in spiritual things. How do you take advantage of life events for the sake of the Gospel?

Second, the purpose of the next section is to prepare you to share the Gospel. A pitfall of more relational style evangelism is that Christians become good at building relationships with lost people, but they never get around to sharing the Gospel. It is imperative that we are not simply trying to enlarge our social circles; we must be true to the calling of Jesus to be His witnesses. To do this effectively, we must know how to transition conversations to the Gospel.

Chapter 5
Connecting to Groups of Lost People – Finding Your Fishing Hole

First Space - Witnessing Where You Live

We now live in a culture where many people no longer know their neighbors. Every day when we come home, we simply open our garage doors, pull inside, and then shut the door behind us. The reality is that there are people literally dying and going to Hell right next door to us and we don't even realize it. Nor, if our actions speak for our hearts, do we really care.

Your neighborhood is a great mission field that needs Christians who are willing to engage their neighbors. Here are some suggestions on how to establish relationships with your neighbors to impact them with the Gospel.

Hospitality

Showing hospitality to your neighbors is a powerful way to establish relationships. Here are some examples of ways to use hospitality:

- **Block Parties**

Block parties are a great way to get to know your neighbors and to begin creating a true community environment within your neighborhood. If you do not know your neighbors, then chances are they also do not know each other. There are some neighborhoods that are exceptions to this, but more and more, people find their fellowship outside of their neighborhood.

A block party is a simple activity to host. Simply create invitations inviting people to come to a cookout. Ask them to bring sides and desserts, while you provide the hamburgers, hotdogs, and drinks. Make sure everyone wears a nametag so that people can begin to learn names. Use the event to establish relationships with your neighbors.

You may be surprised at how much your neighbors would be interested in a block party. I have done a lot of door-to-door ministry in Las Vegas. From door-to-door witnessing to passing out invitations for church events, I've knocked on a lot of doors in the Las Vegas valley. What I found to be so interesting is the reception I received when I went door-to-door in my neighborhood to invite people to a block party. Normally, when going door-to-door, you are met with a great level of suspicion. Sometimes people do not even open the door. Other times they will stand behind their metal security door where you can't see them, but you can hear them. Most people are not very hospitable in these situations. When I went through my neighborhood, however, I had a very different experience. When people first opened the door, they were very cold and distant. The moment I said that I was their neighbor down the street and that I was hosting a block party, the ice melted, and they welcomed me with a warm reception. What I realized through the experience, is that my neighbors wanted to be connected with the people who lived in their neighborhood, but no one was willing to take the lead to bring people together. We had a good turnout for the party and were gifted more bottles of wine than this Baptist preacher had ever had in his house.

- **Dinner Parties**

While a block party is for the entire neighborhood, dinner parties are for one to four families. This allows you to get to know people in a more intimate environment as opposed to the block party, which can have a large crowd. Furthermore, when you invite people into your home for a meal, you begin building a connection. It is interesting that in Luke 10, Jesus instructs the missionaries He was sending out to eat whatever was put in front of them by a city that received them. He was telling them this because he was teaching that a worker is worthy of his wages. I think there was also another important reason for this command. Offering food is an important part of hospitality in most cultures. Turning down food that has been offered is extremely offensive. Food connects people and sharing a meal together creates a wonderful environment to build relationships.

One final note on dinner parties. A goal that you could have is that you start a trend of dinner parties. See if your neighbors would like to do them on a regular basis and if they would like to take turns hosting to share the burden of preparing the meal. Or you can offer to host them on a regular basis but make them a potluck so that everyone contributes.

- **Minister to Your Neighbors**

This past year was extremely challenging for my family. During Thanksgiving of 2023, my mother was admitted to the hospital. While there, the doctors ran several tests, including a biopsy on what appeared to be a tumor on her pancreas. A few weeks later I was sitting with her in a doctor's office waiting to meet with the oncologist. He came in and gave us the news that my mom had pancreatic cancer and that he did not recommend treatment. She was started on hospice care and began the slow decline as the cancer progressed. She passed on June 14, 2024. One of the challenges we faced during those seven months was that my mom and sister lived in Mississippi, but I lived in Nevada. The church I pastor was so gracious to let me go back and forth as often as I needed, but I couldn't be there all the time. My sister had to work as well, and even though she lived with my mom, she couldn't be there twenty-four seven. Fortunately for us, we had wonderful family and friends who stepped in to help. We also had amazing neighbors who ministered and cared for us during that difficult season. They would make sure mom's garbage cans were taken down to the road on trash day and brought back up to the house that evening. If there was something wrong with the house, they were there to help fix it. It seemed like anything we needed our neighbors were ready to serve.

I have known many people in Las Vegas who do not have any family in the city. They often feel alone. They do not have a support structure when crisis hits. What if you were the type of Christian neighbor my mom had? Can you imagine the opportunities you would have to share the Gospel?

Here are some ideas of how you can be a good neighbor and build relationships with lost people:

- Babysit kids

- Mow their lawn

- Celebrate important life events

- Pull their trashcan up the driveway

- Check on your neighbors during bad weather

- Give older neighbors a ride to the doctor

- Prepare food

These are just a few examples of how you can minister to your neighbors. As stated previously, one of the most important parts of living missionally is to be intentional. Start a routine of prayer walking around your neighborhood. As you walk, pray for each house. Pray that God would open doors for ministry. Pray that God would give you eyes to see where He is working so that you may join Him. Pray that you would be sensitive to needs in the community.

Once God starts showing you ways to connect with your neighbors, then it is up to you to take advantage of those opportunities. That will take intentionality and sacrifice. One reason people do not help their neighbors more than they do is because it is often inconvenient. You must be willing to sacrifice your time and resources to be a blessing to your neighborhood.

- **Community Projects**

Organizing community projects can be a great way to connect with your neighbors. Clean-up projects, food/clothes drives, and neighborhood yard sales are all ways to get the neighbors together. Try to organize projects that will lend themselves to having time with your neighbors. For example, while a coat drive might be a worthy cause to help the poor in your community in the winter, it isn't a project that lends itself to people having opportunities to spend time working alongside their neighbors. A clean-up project, however, puts people working closely together for several hours. That would be a better project for promoting relationship building.

- **Start a Neighborhood Bible Study**

Starting a Bible study for your neighbors is a great way to reach them with the Gospel. As you get to know your neighbors, you may find that some of them are interested to learn what the Bible teaches. Starting a weekly Bible study for your neighborhood may be a way to share the Gospel. This strategy does have some challenges. The biggest one is that you do not want to offer a Bible study and just have Christians attend. You can find yourself spending the time you allotted to reach lost people being used up hanging out with more Christians. I am not saying that you shouldn't have any other Christians at the Bible study, but just be aware that the purpose of it is to reach lost people.

If you start a Bible study and it is attended by lost people, don't expect them to act like saved people. You want to create an environment where people feel safe to ask any question. Furthermore, you must work at not being reactive. At a Bible study I led in Las Vegas, that had a high number of lost people attending, guys would use the foulest language you can imagine. The Bible study was definitely not "G" rated. I never once said anything to anyone about cussing. Why? Because cussing was not their problem. It was a fruit issue and not a root issue. Their root problem was that they needed Jesus. I could get them to stop cussing out of shame, but only Jesus could transform their hearts. What is interesting, is that even though I never corrected anyone for cussing, over time, the amount of foul language decreased significantly. Don't get distracted by fruit issues and miss the root problem.

- **Weekly Interest Groups**

The focus of this section has been on how to reach your neighbors. You can also use hospitality to reach people outside of your neighborhood. Targeting your neighborhood is a good place to start if you are not already connected with a good number of lost people. If, however, you are already connected to lost people, you can use your home as a place of ministry to reach them. All the above ideas could be utilized to reach your neighbors or people outside your neighborhood.

The last suggestion I want to recommend is a weekly interest group. People often gather around common interests. By using your home as a place to meet for people to participate in what they are interested in, you are opening the door to build relationships with lost people and share the Gospel. Let me give you some examples of weekly interest groups you could start.

- Sowing / quilting / crocheting
- Cooking
- Classic Car Restoration
- Model Planes
- Poker / Bunco / Other games
- Jiu jitsu / Wrestling
- Scrapbooking
- Card collecting

- Gun customization

- Video games

This list could go on and on forever. What is important to realize, is that you can take an interest that you have and use it as a mission field. Again, you want to make sure that you build into the event time that people can socialize. I have also found that you can often introduce a Bible study as part of the weekly group meeting. Let me share with you three interest groups that I have been a part of.

- **Holy Hold'em**

Years ago, I served on staff at a church where some of the pastors and church leaders would get together on Sunday evenings and play Texas Hold'em Poker. We didn't play for money, but just for fun. We ended up having a guy by the name of Doug Dalton join our game. For those familiar with the poker world, you might recognize his name. Doug was the Director of Poker Operations at Bellagio Hotel and Casino. He designed that poker room and turned it into one of the most successful poker rooms in the world. The high limit room, known as Bobby's Room, was one of the most prestigious places in the world to play poker. Doug had been involved in poker since the 1970's and was probably one of the most famous people in poker from the casino side of the game. He had been a part of the team that codified the rules for Texas Hold'em. He helped start the World Poker Tour. Doug is a legend in the poker world.

The first week Doug joined us he was not impressed. We played on a regular dining room table that was covered with a felt tablecloth. We played a lot of strange variations of poker. We usually had cheap food at the weekly event. The second week Doug came he brought a professional table and took over the food. He also ordered custom poker chips for our game. We still did not play for money, but we did play for prizes and honor. We had a monthly prize for the player with the most chips. If you busted out of chips, you had to wear a goofy hat the rest of the evening and have your picture posted on Facebook.

We quickly realized that though Doug was a believer, he had never been discipled. So, we added Bible study to the event. Each week, we would eat, study the Bible, and then play poker. It was one of the most enjoyable Bible studies I had ever been a part of. We had World Series of Poker Hall of Famers come and play with us. We had a TV crew from ESPN and a famous poker commentator come and film the group. It was a great time of ministry and fun.

- **Jiu Jitsu / Wrestling Bible Study**

When I moved back to Las Vegas in 2011, I became good friend with the Thatcher family. I met them going door-to-door on a short-term mission trip as I prepared to move to Las Vegas to plant a church. The Thatcher family was big into wrestling and jiu jitsu back in those days. Jamie Thatcher coached high school wrestling at a local school here in Vegas. Over the next few years, we became good friends and I ended up renting a room from the Thatchers for a number of years. While living with them, we started a jiu jitsu and wrestling Bible study. We already had people coming over several times a week to train in the garage. We decided to offer a weekly training night that would also include Bible Study. Several of the guys took us up on it and Jamie led the training and I led an evangelistic Bible Study.

What I loved about jiu jitsu is that people seem open to talking about Jesus when you are trying to choke them out. Just kidding. Seriously, jiu jitsu and wrestling seems to be an activity that creates strong friendships. Training hard together. Helping each other improve. Being willing to be the practice dummy as your opponent tries to master a new move helps contribute to an environment of friendship. This then serves as a great opportunity to talk about life and opens the door for the Gospel.

- **Redemption Cigars**

Every week, I have around thirty or so guys come to my house for cigars and Bible study. This is a ministry that started with a third space ministry, which I will share about more in the section on third space ministry, but eventually transitioned into a first space ministry. We have a very simple format; we smoke cigars while studying the Bible. Sometimes we will have food, but it is not every week. While it took a year to find a good day and time to meet, we finally started gaining traction. We have seen a number of men saved and baptized through this ministry.

When I first started the study, I was extremely careful what Christians I invited to be a part of the group. The reason for this, I wanted to reach lost people. The majority of the guys (and few gals) that came to the study were unchurched. This study was not "G" rated. Some of the guys swore like sailors. I had never had so many f-bombs dropped in a Bible study my entire life. The reason I was hesitant to invite Christians is that sometimes they are reactionary towards people like this. I didn't need someone lecturing a lost person on their language. I needed people lovingly showing these guys that they were lost and needed Jesus.

- **Transitioning From One to Another**

I want to point out that the three groups I shared about all began as interest groups. All three were activities that I enjoyed doing, that other people also enjoyed doing, and that could be utilized for the Gospel. It just took a person, or in most cases, a few like-minded people, to take the lead and put the group together. Most people will not initiate a group like this, but they would be happy to join one. You can be the initiator. But what I also want you to see is that we were not satisfied with simply offering an interest group. Both through conversations that we had at the weekly meetings, and by eventually adding Bible studies to the meetings, we started seeing lives changed by the Gospel. The transition to the Bible study was easy because we had laid the groundwork of building relationships with people and speaking truth into their lives from the very beginning.

It is also important to remember that it takes time for groups to gain traction. Sometimes you have to try meeting on a different day. Sometimes you have to try different starting times. Sometimes it just takes a while before people become consistent in attending. Don't give up too quickly just because the group is not growing the way you would like. Also, be sure to encourage the people who attend to recruit other people to join you. Make sure you keep reminding them that this is an open group, and anyone is welcomed and encouraged to join the group.

- **At the Church Campus or in the Home?**

Utilizing interest groups is not a new concept. Churches have utilized this strategy for years. Lots of churches offer basketball leagues, softball leagues, shooting leagues, quilting meetings, and other such interests groups. What I have found, though, is that when you hold it at the church, or make it an official church event, you tend to gather more Christians together than lost people. That is not to say that there haven't been many people saved by these ministries, but I would rather someone start an interest group in his home (first space ministry) or encourage church members to join an interest group that is hosted by someone or some organization in the community (third space ministry) instead of hosting it through the church.

- **Your Home as a Light Upon a Hill**

I hope you can see that using your home as a place of witness is not difficult. It does require a one main thing - intentionally. You must begin being intentional about how you use your home. It seems to me that our culture has moved away from showing hospitality. Our homes have become the place where we hide from the world. It is where we go to get away from people. It seems that more and more we no longer invite people over as much as we use to, but rather, we meet people at other places. Instead of having people over for dinner, we would rather meet at a restaurant. To become effective in using your home as a place of witness you must become intentional about how you use your home. One thing that you and your family can begin praying for is that your home would become a light upon a hill in the neighborhood. Many of your neighbors are living in darkness. They have no clue which way to turn. They have no hope without Jesus. May your house become the beacon of light that shows them the way to hope, peace, and salvation through Jesus Christ.

Chapter 6
Second Space – Witnessing Where You Work

So much of our lives are spent in the places we work. What a waste it would be to spend years working in a place and never see anyone come to faith in Jesus Christ. While your place of employment presents a great field for witnessing, it also presents some challenges. Many places of employment have strict guidelines on proselytizing at work, in which case you must be careful that you are not seen as preaching at work. Though you may not be able to aggressively share the Gospel at work, here are some suggestions on how to have Gospel impact.

- **Be Different**

Your co-workers can sometimes know you as well as your immediate family. They work with you for hours on end every day. They have most likely seen you in stressful situations and in inter-office conflict. It is important, therefore, to establish your credibility as a witness by how you act in the workplace.

- Work hard – Christians ought to be the best employees because they have a Biblical work ethic, which is a strong work ethic. Slacking in your work, or not being a reliable employee, hurts your credibility as a witness for Jesus. Your co-workers should know that you approach your work as if you are working unto the Lord.

- Be truthful – it is amazing how often adults lie to stay out of trouble or to advance themselves. You should be known as a person of truth. Furthermore, people need to know that you are a person of your word. You tell the truth. When you speak, people can trust what you are saying.

- Be kind – Kindness is something missing in many working environments. Because of our sinful nature, people in general, are mean. This is especially true in a competitive environment where people are competing for position, power, and resources. Always being kind and respectful, even in difficult situations, can open the door for Gospel conversations. Let me say this, being kind does not mean that you let people walk all over you, but rather, it means that you always treat people fairly, and that you are in control of your emotions when you speak.

- Avoid Gossip – Gossip abounds in many work environments. Nothing can get people as excited as someone saying, "Did you hear about so and so?" Our flesh loves to gossip. Our flesh loves to hear gossip. We must battle this in our lives. Being a person that is known for Gossip can hinder or even kill our influence for the Gospel.

- Be a person of integrity. It has been said that integrity is doing what is right when no one is watching. You may have known employees that work hard when the boss is around but slack off as soon as he leaves. This type of person lacks integrity. Your co-workers should know that you are the same person no matter who is around. You are not one person around your boss, and another in his absence. You are not one person around certain employees, but someone else around others. Be a person of integrity.

- **Use the "Stones" Strategy**

Many work environments do not allow you to actively proselytize. This does not mean, however, that you cannot be a witness. You are always free to answer questions. The key is getting people to ask the right questions.

I've had the privilege of leading multiple Biblical study tours to Israel. It truly is amazing to travel the Holy Land and read the Bible in the very places where the stories took place. The guy who got me started in leading these tours is a pastor and church planter named George Ross. I remember one time that he was teaching from Joshua 4 and talking about how to use a biblical principle taught in the passage to teach your children about God.

In Joshua 4, God instructs the people of Israel to set up "stones" that mark where the crossing of the Jordan River took place. The reason was so that when future generations asked what those stones meant, it would be an opportunity to share about the works of God. Leading the children to the place of the stones was key in getting them to ask the important questions. This principle is not only good for children but can be used on lost people. The question becomes: "How can you lead people to see the 'stones' in your life?"

- Decorations – Decorations can be a great way to get people to ask questions. A Bible on your desk, a souvenir from a mission trip, a map of a country where your church's missionaries live, or holiday decorations that are distinctly Christian can lead to faith conversations.

- Social media – What you post on social media can directly help or hurt your witness. Utilizing your social media as a missionary tool can open the door for witnessing opportunities at work.

- Speech Seasoned with Grace – While you may not be able to directly witness to co-workers, you can season your words with grace. You can speak of God's grace that sustains you during difficult times. You can share about the great worship experience at church over the weekend. You can offer to pray for those in your office.

- Hospitality – Inviting your co-workers over for dinner or to special events can give you the opportunity to share the Gospel.

While you may face challenges with witnessing at work, the above strategies can help you have impact. While proselytizing may be forbidden at your work, you are allowed to answer questions. By utilizing the above strategies, you can help lead people to ask the right questions that allow you to share the Gospel. Furthermore, building relationships with people at work can give you the opportunity to invite them to the first or third space ministry that you are a part of. Thus, sometimes second space ministry serves as a springboard to get people into another environment where you can openly share the gospel.

When I served in the Middle East, I taught English at various locations in the city where I lived. In those classrooms I had to be extremely careful about sharing the Gospel. Doing so openly would have possibly gotten me arrested, and most assuredly gotten me deported. While I couldn't openly share in the classroom, I could plant seeds of interest by sharing about my family, my travels, and how my faith informed my beliefs about other subjects. Also, being in the classroom gave me the opportunity to hang out in the tea shop each night where I had more freedom to share.

Once again, intentionality is so important. Viewing your workplace as a mission field will change how you approach your job. Just like I recommended prayer walking around your neighborhood, praying regularly for your co-workers is important. Ask God to give you influence and opportunity for the Gospel. Being sensitive to what your fellow employees are going through in their lives can open the door for ministry. The fields at your work are white unto harvest, don't miss the harvest.

Chapter 7

Third Space – Witnessing Where You Play

First and second space ministry is easy to grasp. Everyone knows where they live and where they work. Those are very defined spaces. Third space, however, is not so defined. I define third space as "Where you spend your time between home and work." As I previously mentioned, for many Christians, their only third space is church. If they are not at home or work, then they are probably at church. That is not to say that they never do any other activities, but I mean that they are not regularly apart of anything that doesn't revolve around church. Because of this, many Christians I've pastored really had no clue how to get involved in the community. They are at a lost on how to even get started. Another way to understand what third space ministry is, is to view it as recreational evangelism.

Learning how to use the activities you enjoy as a platform for witnessing is freeing. So often it seems that we make people choose between being involved in church or being involved in recreational activities. We often guilt members into participating in so many different church functions. It seems that the "faithful" are the ones who spend all their free time on the church campus. I believe that Christians should be more involved in community activities as a platform for witnessing.

Utilizing your hobbies and children's activities as platforms to witness can be the most fruitful venues when it comes to sharing your faith. Why not have fun while sharing your faith?

- **Key Aspects of Good Third Space**

Not all third space is equally viable for ministry. You may find that you invest in a third space ministry but never get to meaningful conversations with people, or that you are never talking to the same person twice. There are three main criteria for good third space.

1. A Core Group of People

For a third space to be good for ministry there must be a core group of people involved in the third space. If you are hanging out in a place that has a different group of people there every time you go, then you will never build relationships. You will be starting over each time you visit that third space. You need a group of regulars that you can begin building relationships with and sharing the Gospel.

2. A Consistent Stream of New People

While you need a core group of people, you also need a consistent stream of new people. To refer to the metaphor of the fishing hole, every now and then the hole has to be stocked with fish. If the group is static, then you will reach a point that you are not having any further impact on the Kingdom.

3. Sufficient Socializing Opportunities

The last criterian for a good third space for ministry is that there is sufficient socializing opportunities. The point of participating in these third space activities is so you can start building relationships with lost people. If there is no opportunity to get to know other people, then you are wasting your time.

Evaluating Third Space Opportunities

I want to walk through some potential third space opportunities to see whether they meet the three criteria.

- **Coffee Shop**

I spent a few years training and coaching church planters. One of the topics we would cover is how they were connecting in the community and meeting people. One of the places church planters go to hangout and meet people is a local coffee shop. Most church planters should have a line item in their budget for Starbucks. The question we need to answer is whether a coffee shop is a good third space.

1. A Core Group of People – In my experience, most coffee shops do not have a core group of people that hangout there on a regular basis. While they may have regular customers, it does not seem like a place where everyone knows your name. The planters usually connect with the staff on some level, but it is rare that I have heard of a church planter developing meaningful relationships with patrons. Now this may not be true of every coffee shop, but this has not only been my experience, but also the feedback I have received from multiple church planters throughout the years.

2. A Consistent Stream of New People – A coffee shop does have a steady stream of new people. In an urban environment, people are constantly moving in and out of the area. People change jobs, which brings them into the vicinity of the coffee shop, so there are always new customers.

3. Sufficient Socializing Opportunities – While it seems that a coffee shop would provide a lot of socializing opportunities, that is not often the case. Most coffee shops that you walk into you will find people sitting by themselves, often working or watching something on an electronic device, or you see groups of people who arranged to meet at the coffee shop. What you don't typically see are people who show up without a preplanned meeting socializing with other such people.

After evaluating the three criteria, it seems that a coffee shop is not an ideal third space. While it does have a consistent stream of new people, people do not typically go there to meet people that they are not already scheduled to meet. Also, most coffee shops do not have a strong enough core group of people.

- **Gym**

Another popular place for church planters to go and try and meet people is the local gym. Let's see how it meets the three criteria.

1. A Core Group of People – Gyms typically have a solid core group of people because they usually require membership. The core group changes throughout the day as you have your morning, afternoon, and evening workout people. Some folks love to work out in the morning, others prefer to do it in the afternoon or at night.

2. A Consistent Stream of New People – Gyms do have a consistent stream of new people. This is especially true during the month of January. Those people do not count, however, because they are the New Year's resolution crowd that will be gone by the end of the month. The good news, however, is that the rest of the year provides new people that are joining the gym.

3. Sufficient Socializing Opportunities – While the gym checks the first two boxes, it typically fails on the third. With the advent of earbuds, it seems like everyone is just listening to music as they workout. You do have the guys that go to the gym every day, but don't really workout.

They just hangout. The problem is that there are not enough of them to establish a core group of people.

After evaluating the three criteria, it seems that a gym can be a challenging place to develop third space ministry. Now, I do think there are some ways that you could make it a good ministry space. While most people working out are listening to music and not looking to talk, it could be that by joining one of the group classes you might have opportunities to meet people and start working out together. Also, specialty gyms, such as CrossFit gyms, seem to have more community than regular gyms.

- **Sports League**

Joining a sports league such as softball, bowling, corn hole (yes, that is considered a sports league), target shooting, soccer, pickleball, or any other sports league can be a great way to meet new people. Let's see how well it meets the three criteria:

1. A Core Group of People – Sports leagues, especially team sports, have a solid core group of people. This core can be made up of your teammates or even players on other teams that you see on a regular basis.

2. A Consistent Stream of New People – Notice that this qualification does not say a constant stream, but rather, a consistent stream. I do believe sports teams meet this criterion. While you may not have a constant stream of new people joining your third space, you have a consistent stream. The rhythm of new people may only be at the beginning of each season, but you will typically still have new people joining at regular intervals.

3. Sufficient Socializing Opportunities – The number of socializing opportunities can very between different sports, but for the most part, sports leagues seem to allow for you to get to know people and build relationships.

It seems like sports leagues check all three boxes of the criteria for good third space ministry. Some sports will have more socializing that happens during the game, and some will have less. But overall, this is a good third space ministry.

- **Hiking Groups**

Hiking groups are very popular, especially where you have excellent hiking trails. Let's see how well it meets the three criteria:

1. A Core Group of People – It seems to be that hiker groups have a good amount of regulars to create a core group of people. That doesn't mean that every hiker will sign-up for every hike, yet there are enough regulars to establish a core group.

2. A Consistent Stream of New People – Hiking groups constantly have new people attending the hikes. Each year there seems to be enough new people in the hiking groups to meet the requirement of a consistent stream of new people.

3. Sufficient Socializing Opportunities – Hiking groups have amazing amounts of opportunity to socialize. People usually socialize as they wait to start the hike, talk while hiking, socialize during breaks, and even are prone to hangout for a bit following the hike.

It appears that hiking groups check all three boxes and are excellent places to do third space ministry. They typically give you on average one to four hours per hike and at least once a week to participate. I know many hikers who participate in multiple hikes a week.

- **Sewing Groups**

Many cities have multiple sewing groups you can join. Let's see if they meet the criteria for good ministry space.

1. A Core Group of People – Sewing groups have strong core groups of people. A church I use to serve has a weekly sewing and quilting group. Around 100 women show up each week for several hours. There are also multiple groups throughout the city that meet weekly and are well attended.

2. A Consistent Stream of New People – Sewing groups can have a consistent stream of new people. It may depend on how large the group is and how they advertise the group, but I have seen groups that continue to pick-up new people.

3. Sufficient Socializing Opportunities – This may be one of the best types of groups for socializing. As people work on their projects, they have time to socialize. Also, they are often working on projects together, which helps build friendship and comradery.

Sewing groups check all three boxes and would be a great group to join to pursue third space ministry. Plus, some groups make items to give to people in need. A group that does this would allow you to have strong third space ministry for the Gospel, but also give you an opportunity to meet tangible needs in the community.

Hit or Miss

Determining if a third space is suitable for ministry is not an exact science. I hope the above examples have helped you see how to examine a potential third space environment. Don't be afraid to try out a third space and see if it works. Some of them might surprise you. You may find a coffee shop where people do go to have unscheduled hangouts. You may join a sewing group where no one wants to talk – only sew. You may join a hiking group and realize you are afraid of heights. The point is, try different opportunities, yet evaluate if they seem to be good places to invest your time.

While I have given you several different examples of third space opportunities, there are so many more. Sometimes, however, people have a hard time finding a third space they want to be a part of. Let me give you two tips to help find a third space to pursue. First, write down a list of things you like to do, or maybe things you've always wanted to try. Then look online to see if there are any groups that do those activities. Second, sign-up for websites and apps like meetup.com that specialize in putting groups together. Explore the different groups they offer and give them a try.

Rural Areas

As I was writing this book, it occurred to me that this strategy of third space ministry is more appropriate for urban areas than rural areas. Even though I currently live in Las Vegas, I have spent a good part of my life in small towns and rural areas. The first church I served was a small, country church, twenty minutes from town. The reality for small towns and rural areas is that you do not have as many third space options as cities. While I do believe churches in urban areas should have more streamlined schedules to give its members time to get involved in the community, in rural areas, the church has an opportunity to be the main third space.

In Tate County, Mississippi there is a church called Wyatte Baptist Church. Surprisingly, it is in Wyatte, Mississippi. Wyatte is in the middle of nowhere. There are no stoplights in Wyatte. The only way you know you are there is because of the sign on Hwy 4. The closest town, which only has a population of 10,000 people, is seventeen miles away. About twenty years ago Wyatte Baptist Church called Scott Rogers to be their pastor. When he arrived at the church it ran maybe seventy people on a good Sunday. It was a small, rural church. Under his leadership, the church began offering different activities in the community like Upward Soccer. Over time they started different groups, built a Family Life Center, started an education center, and became the social meeting point of the area. The church grew to approximately 400 in their weekend services.

Wyatte Baptist Church is a great example of how a rural church, that is not competing with a lot of other third space activities, can become the community's third space. I will say, however, that utilizing first space as a ministry hub is still important in rural areas, but a strategy of the church serving the community as the social gathering place is a great way to reach people with the Gospel in a rural setting.

When Your Third Space Picks You

We have spent time looking at how to pick a good third space ministry. The reality for many people, however, is that your third space chooses you. What I mean by this, is that if you are a parent of school-aged children, you often do not have sufficient time to have your own third space ministry. Your children's activities become your third space. That is ok. Many children's activities can serve as a great mission field for third space ministry. The reason for this is because many children's activities check all three boxes of criteria for good third space. The teams and clubs that your children are a part of usually create a good core group of people. As your children grow and progress in their activities, they often join new teams or clubs. During these transitions, they can often keep some of their original core team, while also picking up new people for a consistent stream of new people.

Finally, children's event often provide sufficient socializing opportunities as parents attend practices and games and have a chance to connect with other parents. Furthermore, children often find that their social group is made up of the kids they play on teams with or clubs that they are a part of. So, whether your kids play sports, dance, or are a part of scouting, their activities are often a great place to invest in the Kingdom.

My Third Space Story

About seven years ago I met my friend Doug from my Holy Hold'em group at a local cigar lounge and there I was introduced to the world of cigars. The lounge is located on the west side of Las Vegas. It has an area that is open to the public, but also has a VIP backroom for members. As I started getting more involved in cigars I decided to become a member, and I even got a locker that was two down from OJ Simpson, and three down from another famous actor. I didn't realize it at the time, but I had just found one of the most fruitful fishing holes I've ever encountered.

I realize that some who are reading this book have never been in a cigar lounge. Some of you probably are thinking that you would never darken the door of a cigar lounge. It isn't for everyone, but I have found that cigar longues are great fishing holes. Smoking cigars, for most people, is a social activity. In the craziness of the day, you sit down, light up a stogie, and then spend an hour or so sitting and talking. I have been in cigar longues across the country and around the world. In most of the cigar longues I've visited, I usually end up meeting other people and having good conversation. There have only been a few longues where it did not seem normal for a new person to be welcomed into the group and the conversation. What I also found was that being a member seemed to connect me on a deeper level than just the connection that comes from sharing a love of cigars.

I began spending more and more time at the longue. It became like a second office for me. I would get there in the afternoon and do work on my laptop. I would also hangout in the evenings. I continued to meet more people and became connected to the regulars. I started forming friendships with the members. I also had conversations on everything from sports, local and national politics, family issues – you name it, we talked about it. It was during many of these conversations that I got to share a Biblical worldview on the subject. It was during these conversations that I began to share the Gospel.

In the lounge I met people that fell into one of three categories. There were a few guys who were saved and passionate about Jesus. There were some guys who I believed were saved, but they weren't really walking with the Lord, and it seemed that they had never been discipled. Then there were a lot of lost guys. God was giving me a threefold ministry. For the saved guys who were passionate about Jesus, I was a source of encouragement to them in their walks with the Lord. For the guys who were saved, but not really walking with Jesus, I started trying to disciple them. For the guys who were lost, I took every opportunity I had to share the Gospel.

Over time I started seeing fruit in the lives of the believers who were not really walking with Jesus and in the lives of the guys who were lost. I started a small Bible study with some of the saved guys to help disciple them. Then we started a Bible study to try to reach lost guys and gals who liked cigars. At first, we couldn't gain any traction. We would invite people to the Bible study, yet no one seemed to show up each week. We tried different days, different starting times, but it just seemed to not take root. We did not, however, give up on the idea. Eventually we started having some people show up to the study. We went from three people to five. Then we went from five to about eight. Over time it continued to grow until we had over thirty guys and gals at the study. It got so big that we ended up having to move it from the longue to my RV garage.

One of the interesting things about the Bible study, is that some of the most important conversations I had was not during the actual study time. The important conversations came afterwards when we would just be hanging out and socializing. I had guys opening up about marriage issues, children's issues, and sin problems. It became a place where guys could share about what they were struggling with, and they would receive support, Biblical council, and prayer. We had multiple guys pray to receive Jesus right there in the VIP room at the cigar lounge.

God has done many things through this third space ministry. We have seen a number of guys saved and baptized. We have seen guys set free from various addictions. We have had two marriages saved that looked like they had no hope. Our church has seen new members from this ministry. Even guys who don't go to Redemption have supported us financially. God is continuing to do great things through this ministry as we see new guys come each week and as we work on discipling those who are saved and sharing the Gospel with those who are lost.

Another fruit of the third space ministry is that as of the writing of this book, we are close to launching a video podcast called Redemption Cigars. Ryan, one of the guys who was saved, but not really walking with Jesus, is partnering with me in the venture. Ryan has become passionate about the Lord and seeing people saved. He is a key reason the study has grown and impacted so many people. Together we will launch this podcast that will focus on cigars, Bible study, and interesting people. Our prayer is that it will be a platform that will get the gospel to thousands and thousands of people.

I didn't even know that I had found a fishing hole when I joined the cigar lounge. I just liked cigars, and I enjoyed hanging out at the lounge. What I hope you see through my story, is that you can take what you love to do and use it for the Kingdom. It never ceases to amaze me how God is working in the lives of people and that if I am willing to be used by Him, and I am walking with Him so that I can sense His leadership, He will lead me to people who are open to being saved. We just need to be willing and intentional about how we steward the relationships he has given us. My experience at the cigar lounge has reminded me of a famous saying: "Find a job you love, and you will never have to work a day in your life." Witnessing is not laborious when you are doing in the context of activities that you love and enjoy.

Chapter 8
How to Get Started

Now that we have examined first, second, and third space, you may be asking: "How do I get started?" Let me give you some tips on how to begin engaging your community with the Gospel.

- **Pick a Space**

The first step into engaging your mission field is to pick a space that you are going to target. You can't reach everyone and everywhere at once. So, pray about whether your primary ministry focus should be where you live, where you work, or where you spend your time in between home and work. As stated earlier, these domains sometimes overlap, and that is ok; but you need to decide which area is going to be your focus.

If you are going to use your first space (where you live) as your primary ministry platform, then you must decide if you are primarily going to target your neighbors, or if you are going to target people outside of your neighborhood. If you are targeting your neighbors, then you will look for ways to get the neighbors together and to minister to your neighbors. If you're targeting people outside of your neighborhood, then you may start an interest group at your house.

Most people cannot use their work as a primary target area. They have too many restrictions. You, however, may be the exception to this. If so, then you need to begin praying for your co-workers and customers and begin seeing how you can develop deeper relationships and utilize opportunities to speak the Gospel. If you are not able to make this your primary target, you can still do some of the suggested activities previously covered.

For those who are going to utilize third space for your focus, then you may have to start testing and evaluating different third spaces. Some may work well for you, while others may not prove to meet the criteria needed to build strong third space ministry. Also, you may use this as an opportunity to try new hobbies or sports. You may find a third space that is good for ministry, but you realize you don't enjoy the activity tied to it. That is ok, you can try something else. I think it is important to find something you enjoy doing and that gives you ministry out-reach. That is where you will thrive the most.

- **Teamwork is Biblical**

There are three passages that I think are important to reflect on as we strategize on how to engage lostness.

- Luke 9:1-2 – "And he called the twelve together and gave them power and authority over all demons and to cure diseases, and he sent them out to proclaim the kingdom of God and to heal."

- Luke 10:1-2 – "After this the Lord appointed seventy-two others and sent them on ahead of him, two by two, into every town and place where he himself was about to go"

- 1 Corinthians 12:18-20 – "But as it is, God arranged the members in the body, each one of them, as he chose. [19] If all were a single member, where would the body be? [20] As it is, there are many parts, yet one body."

There are two primary lessons I want you to see from the three passages. First, Jesus did not send the missionaries out on their own. He sent the twelve out to-gether, and then he sent the seventy-two out two by two. Also, we see in Paul's ministry that he always had other believers around him helping him in the work God had called him to do. Second, Jesus has given the body (the church) various members who are designed and gifted to serve in different rolls. These differences are important, because they complement each other and allow the body to func-tion properly.

Now, how do these two lessons apply to missional living? First, God has called us to serve with other Christians. I think there are several reasons why this is wise. When you engage in ministry you are engaging in spiritual warfare. The enemy will try to cause you to stumble and fall. This can be in the form of leading you into false teaching, or by trying to get you into sin. Having another believer beside you in ministry helps give you accountability. Also, it gives a double witness as lost people see two lives that have been changed by the Gospel and hear about how

Jesus has impacted each of you. Furthermore, the two of you will have different giftings that can complement each other in reaching people with the Gospel.

So, as you begin to engage your community, seek a fellow believer to serve with you. Support each other, pray for each other, and serve alongside each other. This is the Biblical model that we see in the New Testament both with how Jesus sent people into the harvest and how Paul operated as the church expanded throughout the world.

- **Prioritize Your Schedule**

I think one of the major challenges for people to be effective in reaching their communities with the Gospel is time. We live such busy lives, where we are constantly on the go and do not have time to invest in lostness. Developing first or third space ministry takes a time commitment. To be effective, you may have to change how you utilize your time. I know some folks that are involved in three or four different Bible studies a week. For them to be effective, they may have to cut down to one Bible study a week so that they have time to be involved in evangelism. Other people are so busy doing family events that they have no time for ministry. They are so busy making memories that they are having no impact for the Kingdom. I would recommend making memories that last for eternity. Figure out how you can do things with your family as you seek to reach lost people. I also know some families that have their children in so many activities that they spend all their days running from one activity to the other. Somehow people have come to believe that being a good parent means having your children in every single activity they want to do. Children do not have to be involved in so many activities to have a good and healthy childhood. Training children from a young age that Jesus is Lord of our schedule is important. That means that we dedicate an appropriate amount of time to what He has called us to do.

I cannot stress enough that I think an important way to prioritize (or manage) your time is to be disciplined to use a calendar. They say that as you get older time goes by faster. It seems like you blink, and half the year has passed. If you are not intentional about calendaring your time, then you will miss ministry opportunities. Calendaring allows you to build in space for ministry by blocking time out for investing in peoples' lives. This is especially true if you have children. It seems like keeping everyone's schedule sorted is a full-time job. Utilize a calendar as a part of intentional missional living.

- **Walk with Jesus**

No ministry is a substitute for intimacy with Jesus. It is imperative that we are walking with the Lord if we are going to have Kingdom impact. John 15:5 says: "I am the vine; you are the branches. Whoever abides in me and I in him, he it is that bears much fruit, for apart from me you can do nothing." In this passage, Jesus teaches that we must abide in Him for two reasons. First, it is only in abiding in Him that we will bear much fruit. Second, apart from Him we can do nothing. So, if we want to be fruitful in ministry, then we must maintain our walk with Jesus. It is so easy to get busy with ministry and neglect our relationship with Jesus.

While we need to practice all the Spiritual Disciplines, it is important that we spend sufficient time in prayer and time in the Word. It is through these two disciplines that the Lord will guide us to where He is working. One of the guys that hung out at my third space was a successful businessman. This is a guy that I had gotten to know over a few years, but we were not close. We had enjoyed multiple conversations in group settings, but we never really hung out together. I started praying for him whenever I saw one of his company's work vans or advertising signs. I had been doing this for months when one day as I was praying for him, I felt the Lord impress upon me that I needed to tell the guy I was praying for him. Later that night I was driving home, and I felt a burden to go to the cigar lounge and hangout. I was ready to go home, but I obeyed what I sensed was the leading of the Lord. When I arrived at the cigar lounge, the back room for members was closed with a sign on the door that indicated there was a private party happening. So, I sat in the general area and just waited. A few minutes later the private party in the back room ended and people started coming out to leave. The guy I had been praying for came out of the back room and when he saw me, he came over and sat down to talk. I think that may have been the first time we had ever sat and talked without a larger group around us. After a little bit of conversation, he told me it was getting late and he had to get home. I told him that before he left, I wanted him to know that any time I see one of his company vans or see an advertisement that I pray for him. I then asked him if there was anything I could specifically be praying for in his life. That one night opened the door for multiple Gospel conversations with this man. I truly believe that if I had not been walking with the Lord, I would not have recognized His leading and would have missed the opportunity to share the Gospel with this guy.

I learned an important lesson early on in ministry. When I was a college student I was also serving a local church. I was hired as the youth minister and then later was promoted to Associate Pastor of Youth. Both our music minister and our senior pastor left the church, and I was the only staff member left. I found myself as the interim pastor, worship pastor, and youth pastor of a small country church. I was doing all of this while still a full-time student in college. It was a really busy season. During that time, I stopped being consistent in having a daily devotional time with the Lord. If you had asked me if I was in the Word daily, I would have emphatically said yes, because I was. During that season I was preaching a Sunday morning service, a Sunday night service, leading youth Bible study, and preaching at other events as opportunities arose. I was in the Word every day because I was preparing to preach or teach multiple times a week.

After a while I found myself feeling spiritually drained. It is like my spiritual gas tank was on empty. The Lord convicted me that I had been slacking on my devotional time with him. What I realized is that there is a huge difference between being in the Word to prepare to preach or teach and being in the Word for devotional purposes. My motive for being in the Word when I'm preaching a sermon or lesson is to be well prepared. That is not a bad motive. God has called preachers to be prepared. My motive for time in the Word during my devotional time is that I want to spend time with Jesus. That is a very different motivation for being in the Word. The first is ministry, which is a good thing, but not the ultimate. The second is for relationship. Be careful not to forsake your relationship with Jesus because you are so busy doing ministry. Do not make the mistake that preparing to witness, teach, or preach can replace time in the Word that is focused on spending time with Jesus.

- **Develop a Biblical Worldview**

A few times in this book I have mentioned that churches often overschedule activities. I've stated that some people need to cut back on the number of Bible studies they attend to have time to invest in lostness. My fear is that you as the reader will think I do not believe the Word of God is important. I want to clearly state that the Word is of upmost importance in being the witness Jesus has called you to be. One of the things you need to do as you engage lostness through first, second, or third space ministry is to really ensure that you have a Biblical worldview and that you can articulate why you believe what you believe.

You may be asking: "What is a worldview?" Everybody has a worldview, even though they may not realize it. Think of a worldview as a pair of invisible glasses you are always wearing. Through the lenses of the glasses, you view everything that happens around you. Those lenses shape everything that you see. Your culture, religious beliefs, family background, and education all have shaped your worldview. As you look at events that happen around you, your worldview shapes them and helps you understand and interpret them.

Two people with different worldviews can see the exact same thing yet interpret them differently. Let me give you a few examples. Imagine you see two grown men walking down the street holding hands. According to your western worldview, you would probably assume that they are homosexuals. It is not normal in our culture for two heterosexual men to walk down the street holding hands. If someone from the Middle East saw the two men, he might assume they are just good friends. In the Middle East, it is common for men who are simply friends to show physical affection towards one another by holding hands as they walk. There is nothing sexual about it. That practice, however, goes totally against a Western worldview. I remember that before I moved to the Middle East I had gone through extensive training on their culture and worldview. I knew that it was perfectly normal for grown men to hold hands while walking down the street. One day I was out with some of my local friends. I was trying to fit into the culture, so I was wearing national dress, which was what I called a man skirt. So, there I was, a little uncomfortable wearing a skirt, walking down the street with a friend who suddenly reached out and started holding my hand as we walked. I remember thinking: "Here I am walking down a public street, wearing a skirt, holding hands with another man – missions really changed my life!" It was very uncomfortable for me. Even though I had been trained that this was ok, and it had no sexual meaning, my worldview was screaming in my head that this was wrong!

Imagine that you are living somewhere in Africa. You have an appointment with someone at a tea shop at 3:00pm. Being from America, you believe in being punctual. You arrive at 2:55. You order some tea and wait for your friend to arrive. 3:00 comes and goes. It is now 3:10 and you keep checking your phone to see if your friend has sent you a text message. 3:15 then passes, and it is now 3:20. You are irritated. How rude for your friend not to let you know that he is running late. You think to yourself that it better be an emergency to be that late. Then you think, "Maybe he forgot." Right as you are finally about to text him to see if he is coming, he walks up at 3:25. You stand up to greet him and the two of you sit down. He also orders a tea and begins to chat with you. You are sitting there waiting for him to apologize for being late, but he never does. You find yourself trying to concentrate on the conversation, but you are angry that he would so disrespect your time. Why is he not apologetic for being late? The reason? In his worldview he is not late. His culture does not value being punctual, but rather making sure you greet people. Also, he arrived at 3:25, which in his worldview is still 3:00. He would only be late if he arrived after 4:00.

These two examples show differences between very different worldviews. When you are ministering within your culture, you are ministering to people who have a much similar worldview to you. While it may be similar, it is not the same. They may have grown up in a different part of the city, state, or country than you. They had a different family background. They have a different religious background. All of these things shape your worldview. Though many things within your worldview are the same, these differences can cause you to have very different beliefs on many different issues.

As you develop relationships you are going to engage people in a lot of conversation. You will most likely talk about all sorts of issues. Politics, morality, rearing children, public policy, and current events are all topics that will come up as you spend time with lost people. It is in these conversations that you can season your words with grace and help open the door to the Gospel. When someone asks me what I think about an issue, I usually respond that I try to base everything I believe on the Bible. I try to have a biblical worldview. So, if it is a moral issue, I want to know what the Bible says about that issue. If it is a political issue, I want to see how the teachings of the Bible should direct my position. By reminding people, in a humble way, that the Bible is your foundation for what you believe, it will open the door for the Gospel. But to be able to do this, you have to know how the Bible speaks to these issues. You must be in the Word and constantly searching the Word to find a Biblical worldview that you can share with people in your ministry areas.

- **Be Proficient in Sharing the Gospel**

Sharing the Gospel is essential in having successful evangelistic ministry. It doesn't matter if you are the king or queen of hospitality. It doesn't matter if you find the most amazing third space ministry location or activity. It doesn't matter if you are able to connect deeply with lost people. If you do not know how to share the Gospel, then you are not going to have much Kingdom impact. To do this, you need to be proficient in sharing the Gospel. While this book gives training in how to do it, it takes more than just reading about witnessing to become proficient in witnessing. That would be like reading a book on how to play golf and thinking you can play well. So how do you become proficient in witnessing? By following two easy steps.

First, you need to learn how to share the Gospel. Again, this book teaches you how to use your testimony and the Bible to witness. This will require that you do the work of writing out your testimony and memorizing it so that you can easily share it. It will also require that you learn the passages to use from the Bible in a witnessing encounter. All of that is here in this book, but you must take the time and make the effort to learn it.

Second, like with any other skill, you need to practice. I learned an important lesson from my friend and leadership expert, Mac Lake. He says, "Practice doesn't make perfect. Evaluated practice makes perfect." So, as you begin to practice, you need to find someone with experience witnessing and practice with him or her. Let that person coach you on how you are witnessing. When I teach people how to share their testimony as a witness, I then give them an assignment to first share it with three "safe" people. A safe person is someone that is a believer. That way the believer can give feedback on how easy it was to understand the testimony. Once you have become comfortable sharing with safe people, then you have to start sharing it with lost people.

I also think that a great way to become comfortable in witnessing is to do some drive-by witnessing. Go to a public park, a mall, or anywhere else people hangout and try to engage strangers with the Gospel. While this may scare you, it will give you reps that will help you become more confident in sharing.

Sometimes people tell me that it is so easy for me to witness. What they don't understand is that it has not always been so easy. When I first started sharing my faith, I found myself scared to death. I would stumble through the presentation, sometimes forgetting what verse came next. Over time, however, I became more and more comfortable sharing as I became more and more proficient. In seminary I use to lift weights at a local high school with a buddy of mine. He helped coach football at the high school and knew all of the students. Usually we went at night, but sometimes we would go during the afternoon. When we were there in the afternoon, some of the students would be in the weight room lifting. A lot of the younger ones would try to lift weights that they were not strong enough to lift. They would compromise their form in order to lift the weight. Not only does this reduce the effectiveness of the lift, but it can also lead to injury. My friend would always go up to them and tell them to get a lighter weight. Then he would tell them a statement that has stayed with me all these years. "It doesn't matter where you start, it matters where you finish." If you are just beginning your journey as a witness for Jesus, don't worry about if you are not super proficient. The more you share, the more proficient you will get. Embrace the newness of witnessing and keep focused on become better at sharing the Good News of Jesus Christ.

Biblical Prayer

Ephesians 6:12 states: "For we do not wrestle against flesh and blood, but against the rulers, against the authorities, against the cosmic powers over this present darkness, against the spiritual forces of evil in the heavenly places." It is important to remember that when you share the Gospel, you are engaging in spiritual warfare. Satan and his forces are fighting for the souls of men, women, boys, and girls. He wants as many people as possible to remain separated from God. As previously discussed, we are engaged in a war against the kingdom of Hell. We are to storm the gates and take the victory. Just because we know that the gates of Hell cannot stand against us, does not mean that they will not put up a fight. We must be faithful to spend time on our knees in this battle against Satan. It is not our ability to clearly articulate the Gospel, nor our proficiency at developing good first or third space ministry that will see lives changed; it is the power of God that saves people. We can do nothing of eternal significance on our own. We need the Lord.

It is so easy for our prayer life to be centered on temporary things. We pray for our health, our families, our jobs, for things that we want or think we need. What I find interesting, is that most of Paul's prayers were centered on thanksgiving and the work of the ministry. For example, look at what Paul wrote to the believers in Colossae in Colossians 4:2-4: "Continue steadfastly in prayer, being watchful in it with thanksgiving. [3] At the same time, pray also for us, that God may open to us a door for the word, to declare the mystery of Christ, on account of which I am in prison— [4] that I may make it clear, which is how I ought to speak." As Paul mentions in that passage, he is in prison for preaching the Gospel. Paul asks the church to pray for him, but not in the way that I would probably ask. If I were in prison and was asking a church to pray for me, I think I would ask them to pray that I would be freed from prison. I would ask them to pray that I would have a good attorney, that the food would be better, that I wouldn't have a scary cell mate. I think I would be so overwhelmed by my circumstances, that I would be praying for that which benefits me. Paul, however, did not ask for prayer for his personal freedom or comfort. He did not ask for God to change his circumstances, but rather, that God would use his circumstances to further the Gospel. Paul asked the church to pray for an open door to share the Gospel. This is so counter cultural to what I find in most church prayer meetings I've attended throughout my life.

Our prayer life should be centered on God's Kingdom. Too often, our prayer life is centered on our kingdom. In Matthew 6:33, Jesus said: "But seek first the kingdom of God and his righteousness, and all these things will be added to you." He tells us that we are to seek first the kingdom of God. The priority of our prayer life should be centered around the Kingdom of God, not our circumstances. I have attended a lot of Wednesday night prayer meetings in many different churches. When I am visiting a church, I like to see if they have a prayer guide available. What I have found is that many churches spend most of their energy praying for temporary things. They are praying for people's health, finances, and job situations. I used to call the Wednesday night prayer meeting the weekly health update. Little to no time was spent praying for lostness. This type of praying is not seeking first the Kingdom of God.

Now, let me say that I am not against praying for healing, finances, and other life issues. I do believe that we are to lift these things up to the Lord. Matthew 6 shows us that these things are important to God. The reason we are not to put these issues as our primary focus in prayer is because Jesus tells us that He will provide those things. When the verse says "and all these things will be added unto you" Jesus is referring to the necessities of life. We don't have to focus on them because Jesus has those issues already covered.

When we pray, we need to have an eternal perspective, even when praying for the necessities of life. For example, when I am praying for a fellow believer who is sick, I ask that the Lord may heal him. I also pray that though he may be physical weak because of the illness, that he would be spiritually strong and that through this circumstance, he may have opportunity to be a witness for Jesus. That as he sits in waiting rooms to see doctors, he might get to share the hope that he has with people who are going through similar situations, but without any hope. When someone is praying for a job, I ask that the Lord not only provide him a job that would meet his daily needs, but one that would give him a great mission field for the Gospel. Praying like this keeps you focused on the Kingdom of God and not on your circumstances.

Praying for Lostness

As you begin developing ministry in either your first, second, or third space, you want to develop a consistent prayer time for that ministry. I want to suggest things you should include in your prayers.

1.   Sensitivity to Where God is Working

As we already talked about, the Bible uses the illustration of a harvest when it comes to winning people to Jesus. If you have ever had a garden, you know that fruit ripens at different times. One day you go outside to your garden, and you may only have one tomato that is ready to pick. The next day you may have two. Each plant produces fruit that ripen at different times. The same is true with people and being saved. Sometimes I share the Gospel with someone one time and they are ready to be saved. Others have taken time and multiple conversations before they were ready to trust in Jesus.

We need to ask God to give us sensitivity to where He is working so that we may join Him in His work. If we are trying to see where God is working with our physical eyes, we will often miss what he is doing. Had Samuel just used his physical eyes in looking at Jesse's sons, he would have missed who God had chosen to be king. He would have picked one of David's brothers, but he was walking with the Lord and entuned with His leadership. Had Ananias only seen Saul with his physical eyes, he would never have laid hands on him and healed him. It was only because Ananias knew that God was working in Saul's life, and at the Lord's command, that he went to Saul. These two examples show us that God is often working in the lives of people that we would not expect. My friend Ryan, who started the cigar Bible study with me, had a friend that he wanted to invite to the study. He was nervous about asking the friend. The guy was a successful businessman, never seemed to show interest in spiritual things, and came from a Mormon background. Despite his fear, Ryan asked his friend. Not only was the friend interested in checking out the Bible study, but he started coming every week. God had already been working in his life, and he eventually gave his life to Jesus.

Unless we are prayerfully walking with God, and obeying His leading, we will miss divine appointments that He has for us. We need to consistently ask the Lord to show us where He is working so that we may join Him.

2. Favor with People

At the end of Acts 2, the Bible records how the early church was functioning and how they were reaching people with the Gospel. It states in verse forty-seven: "praising God and having favor with all the people. And the Lord added to their number day by day those who were being saved." Part of what was leading to people being saved is that they had favor with all the people. God gave the believers favor in their communities with the lost people around them. As we begin developing ministry in our various spaces, we should ask God to give us favor with people. That word favor in the original Greek means grace. Grace is unmerited favor. God can turn people's hearts towards us so that they immediately give us favor without having to earn it.

One of the things that has amazed me in the ministry the Lord called me to in Las Vegas, is how many influential and affluent people I have met. People usually associate with people who are in the same place in life and in a similar socio-economic level. When I started hanging out at the cigar lounge in Vegas, I quickly found myself around a lot of wealthy and influential people. I would always joke that I was the poorest guy in the cigar lounge. What was amazing, however, is that God seemed to give me favor with the other members. While my extensive travels throughout the world, and my level of education helped to bridge some of the social gaps that come with being in very different socio-economic tiers, I believe that God gave me favor with people who live very different lifestyles than myself. Because of that favor, I've had many opportunities to share the Gospel with people from very different backgrounds in my city.

3. Opportunities to Share

Have you ever watched someone force a witness? I have seen people who so wanted to share the Gospel that they forced the conversation. It was obvious that the person didn't want to listen, yet the person kept on sharing. That can be a painful thing to watch. We don't want to force the Gospel on anyone. We should never be slow to share, but we should also be asking the Lord to give us clear opportunities with people who are willing to listen. It is amazing how God can orchestrate opportunities for us if we wait on Him and ask Him. One such example that comes to mind is the Philippian jailor in Acts 16.

In a dream, Paul had been instructed by the Lord to go to Macedonia instead of Asia. Obeying the leading of the Lord, Paul and Silas found themselves in Philippi. While there, they cast a demon out of a slave woman who made her owners a lot of money fortunetelling. Seeing that they had lost a significant source of income, her owners stirred up trouble for Paul and Silas, who were beaten and then thrown into jail. About midnight, Paul and Silas were praying and singing hymns. What is interesting is that the Bible clearly says that the prisoners were listening. The prison guard, however, was not listening. He was busy sleeping. Suddenly there was a mighty earthquake that shook the very foundation of the prison. During this earthquake all the prison doors opened. Startled by the earthquake, the prison guard woke up and saw that the doors were open. He immediately assumed that all the prisoners had fled the prison. Thinking this, he grabbed his sword and was about to kill himself. He figured it would be easier for him to kill himself than allow the Romans to kill him for failing at his job. Suddenly, Paul yells out to the guard informing him that none of the prisoners had escaped. They were all still sitting in their cells. The guard then brought Paul and Silas outside of the jail and asked them what he needed to do to be saved. Paul and Silas shared the Gospel, and the man received Jesus. Not only did he receive Jesus, but he took them to his house and the rest of his family became believers. They were all baptized that same night.

What took that prison guard from a place of disinterest in what Paul and Silas were talking about to wanting to know how to be saved? It was a work of God in his life. Sometimes God has to shake up a person's life to bring him to a place where he is ready to listen. Asking God to give you opportunities to share the

Gospel is asking God to do a work in people's lives that bring them to the point that they are ready and willing to hear.

One last thing I want to point out about this story is that Paul and Silas did not wait to start talking about Jesus until the man asked, but as they shared with other people, this guy probably heard some of the conversations. He just wasn't really interested. However, the seeds they sowed as they shared the Gospel, prayed, and worshiped God, bore fruit in this man's life when God did a work to open his heart to the Gospel. There are those who believe that you have to spend a long time developing a relationship with someone before you can share the Gospel. I don't necessarily agree. I believe that you can talk about Jesus from the very beginning. That doesn't mean that you go into a full-blown witness presentation, but that you season your words with grace. Also understand that as you do have opportunities to share with people within your ministry space, other people may hear and be impacted by the Gospel. There is a time for sowing and a time for reaping. Be faithful in sowing and opportunities to reap will come.

4. Knowledge and Wisdom

The longer I have worked with people the more I have learned that people are messy. This is true whether you are talking about people in the church or people outside of the church. We all deal with sin in our own lives and in the lives of people around us. As you connect with people on a deeper level, you will find that they often will share their messiness with you and seek your council on what to do. Some of the situations will be the result of the individual's sin. Some will be about someone else's sin that is impacting his life. Some will be about issues that arise from living in a fallen world. Sometimes people's lives seem so entangled by sin that you're not sure where to even begin to help them get free. It is during encounters like this that you need two things. First, you need knowledge. Knowledge is having the facts and information to know what is right. For this, you need the Bible. What does the Bible specifically say about what the person is going through, or what principles apply to his situation? This is why we must be faithful to continually study and know the Word of God. We should seek to live up to Paul's exhortation to Timothy in 2 Timothy 2:15 when he says: "15 Do your best to present yourself to God as one approved, a worker who has no need to be ashamed, rightly handling the word of truth."

The second thing we need is wisdom. The question is, what is the difference between knowledge and wisdom? Think of it this way – knowledge is knowing where you need to be, wisdom is knowing how to get from where you are to where you need to be. Wisdom is the application of knowledge. It takes wisdom to know how to apply the Bible to a person's life. Again, sin is entangling. Sometimes it seems like a person is so entangled that there is no way out without violating some Scriptural command.

The Bible gives us a wonderful promise about wisdom. James 1:5 says: "If any of you lacks wisdom, let him ask God, who gives generously to all without reproach, and it will be given him." God has promised to give us wisdom if we simply ask Him. The question is, how does He give us wisdom? Biblically, I think there are several ways that He gives us wisdom. First, He gives us wisdom through His Word. There have been times that God has reminded me of a story in the Bible that helped give me wisdom on how to counsel a person. Second, He gives us wisdom through the counsel of Godly men and women. Sometimes, instead of immediately giving someone counsel, we need to ask him to give us time to pray over the matter and seek counsel. We then should seek out Godly men and women and see what sort of wisdom they might have to share with us. I think Acts 15 is an example of this when the Jerusalem Council met to discuss whether or not gentiles needed to be circumcised. Furthermore, I think this is why you see a plurality of leadership in churches, so that Godly men can search the Scriptures together and seek wisdom as a team.

I think a third way that God gives wisdom is supernaturally on the spot. Jesus told His followers in Matthew 10:19: "When they deliver you over, do not be anxious how you are to speak or what you are to say, for what you are to say will be given to you in that hour." This is an example of God giving a believer wisdom in the moment. I have experienced this at times, but I have also found that God has given me wisdom through the other means listed. Whichever way He chooses, we simply have to ask, and He gives it liberally and without reproach.

5. Individuals

Finally, we need to pray for individuals on a regular basis. As you begin to connect with the lost people in your fishing hole, begin praying for them regularly. You can pray for them each day during your daily quiet time. You can pray for them before each of your events where you will see them. Praying for the lost people in your fishing hole is a great family activity. Each night before your kids go to bed, have a family devotion time that ends with prayer for the people each of you are trying to reach with the Gospel. If bedtime doesn't work, do it as you drive them to school each morning. It never ceases to amaze me that when I regularly pray for people that I see God open doors for the Gospel.

You may be asking how you should pray for people. Pray for opportunities to share. Pray that God would bring them to a place where they are open to the Gospel. Pray that God would give you opportunities to minister to them in special ways. Pray that God would give you wisdom to speak truth into their lives. Pray that they may see God's love through how you minister and speak to them.

I cannot emphasize enough the power of letting people know that you pray for them daily or at least regularly. Imagine you are at the baseball field watching your son or daughter play, and you are speaking with another parent. You tell the parent that every night before your kids go to bed, you pray for each family by name. Just think about the impact that could have on that parent. Also, that creates a wonderful opportunity to ask if that family has any specific prayer requests. This question can open all sorts of ministry opportunities and Gospel conversations. Be sure that you write down the prayer requests, pray for them, and follow-up with the family to let them know that you really are praying for them.

I have seen people soften to the Gospel because they found out that I pray for them. I've seen them seek me out when God is shaking up their lives because they know I pray for them. Even people that are not sure God exists have usually appreciated that I am praying for them. I have been asked, "How are you praying for me?" I usually respond that I am praying for God's blessings on their lives and that they would know how much He loves them.

6. Passion

While fear may be one of the major reasons people do not witness, apathy is either the top reason or it comes in at a close second. For many Christians, they just do not have a passion to see lost people saved. I have seen this throughout my ministry. If a pastor offers a class on the book of Revelation, you will fill the classroom. If you offer a class on witnessing, it usually has much lower attendance. Two passages come to mind about the type of passion that we should have over lostness. The first is Matthew 9:36-38: "When he saw the crowds, he had compassion for them, because they were harassed and helpless, like sheep without a shepherd.

"Then he said to his disciples, 'The harvest is plentiful, but the laborers are few; [38] therefore pray earnestly to the Lord of the harvest to send out laborers into his harvest.'"

In this passage Jesus has just been traveling throughout the cities and villages. He had been teaching and healing the sick. He then looks upon the crowds and is moved with compassion because they were in a desperate situation. He said that they were harassed and helpless. He then goes on to say that they were like sheep without a shepherd. Sheep that do not have a shepherd are destined for destruction. They have no natural way to protect themselves. What Jesus was saying is that the multitudes were lost and without hope. Seeing this, the Bible says that Jesus was moved with compassion. I wonder, when is the last time you have been emotionally moved by compassion for the lost? When is the last time you have driven down your street and wondered how many of your neighbors are dying and going to Hell? How many times have you looked at the other families involved in your children's activities and wondered how many of them are dying and going to Hell?

Why are we so apathetic to lostness? Maybe it is because we really don't believe people will spend eternity in Hell separated from God. Maybe it is because we have just been so habituated to lostness that we don't even notice it anymore. Maybe we are just so busy living our lives we do not care because of distraction. When is the last time that you obeyed Jesus' command to pray that God would thrust out laborers into the harvest? The compassion Jesus experienced was not just a passing emotion, but a compassion that led Him to die for the sins of the world. We do not need a compassion that impacts us for a moment, but an ongoing compassion that moves us into the action of sharing the Gospel.

You may be thinking, "Of course Jesus had compassion, He is God." Well, there is another example of great passion for lostness in the New Testament. Romans 9:1-3 states: "I am speaking the truth in Christ—I am not lying; my conscience bears me witness in the Holy Spirit— [2] that I have great sorrow and unceasing anguish in my heart. [3] For I could wish that I myself were accursed and cut off from Christ for the sake of my brothers, my kinsmen according to the flesh." Here Paul makes an extremely bold statement. Basically, he says that he wishes that he could be condemned to Hell if it meant that his fellow Jews could be saved. What a passion Paul had for lostness! Again, Paul's compassion for lostness was not just a passing emotion, but rather, an ongoing driving force for how he lived his life.

As you pray for lostness, you may need to admit to the Lord that you lack passion for lost people. It is important that we remember that we cannot will ourselves to be who God desires us to be, but we can surrender to Jesus and ask Him to change our hearts. As you consistently pray for lost people, as you ask for God to give you a greater passion for lostness, and as you begin to obey God's calling for you to be His witness, God will increase your awareness of lostness and your compassion for their situation and a passion to give them hope that only comes through the Gospel.

Chapter 9
Getting the Conversation Started

Some people naturally have the gift of gab. They can and will start up a conversation with anyone at any time. When I think of people like this, my mind immediately goes to a man who was named Paul Hall. Mr. Paul, as I knew him, was good friends with my dad. He and his wife, Oliva, went to the same church as my parents. We often would go out to eat with the Halls. By the time we had eaten dinner and walked out of the restaurant, Mr. Paul would have talked to at least half a dozen people that he didn't know. He was not shy and could start a conversation with anyone. Not everyone has this gift. I recently had a man tell me that he has a hard time having conversations with people that he doesn't know well or people that have different interests than him. This is a common challenge for people. The key to starting conversations is to lead with questions. People often enjoy talking about themselves. They really open up when people seem to take a genuine interest in them and their lives. By asking people questions, it shows that you have an interest in knowing them and it can usually get a good conversation going.

One important key to asking questions, is to start with casual conversations. It is important that you do not start with too heavy of a conversation or anything that is too personal. You want them to think that you are a friendly person, not a creep. You also want to avoid controversial subjects. Questions about one's political views usually are not good lead off questions. Let me give you come categories of questions that you can work through as you transition from casual conversation to the Gospel.

1. Interests

If you are following the strategy of this book, then you are probably meeting lost people at some sort of activity or interest group. This provides you with a great category of questions to engage people in conversation. Start with the activity or interest that brought you together. For example, if you have just joined a bowling league, you can ask someone how long he has been bowling. This can lead to a host of follow-up questions:

- What got you into bowling?

- How long have you been a part of this league?

- What drew you to this league?

- How has league bowling helped to improve your game?

These are just a few examples of questions that you can ask about the interest. Each question can lead to conversation as you talk about your experience with the activity.

2. Background

From interests, it is really easy to move to background. One of the advantages about living in Las Vegas, is that it seems that most people are originally from somewhere else. Background questions can include:

- How long have you lived here?

- Where are you from originally?

- What brought you here?

- How do you like this area?

- What do you miss about where you came from?

- What was it like growing up here?

- Has the area changed a lot?

3. Current Situation

Once you have covered interests and background you can move to their current situation. This gets more personal, but you should have already started building enough rapport to ask these questions. Here are some that you can ask:

- Are you married?

- Do you have any kids?

- What do you do for a living?

- What other interests do you have?

- Do you go to church anywhere? If so, where?

Building Relationships

One of the goals as you connect with lost people is to build relationships. It starts with conversation but requires more than just casual conversation to go deeper. Some activities and spaces allow for deeper conversations, others not so much. For example, the cigar longue provided a great environment for long, deep conversations. Not all conversations were deep, but there were many that focused on important issues in life. The nature of a cigar longue is to sit and have long talks. Other activities, however, may not provide opportunities for long conversations. Being a part of a sports team may give you time to chat, but because you are playing a sport you may not have time to get into deeper conversations. In those situations, you must take steps to move those relationships from being casual to deeper.

Getting to deeper relationships takes time and intentionality. I've found that some people are natural inviters. They are the people that are naturally gatherers of people. Others, however, rarely invite others to do things or host people. No matter which category you fall into, to build deeper relationships you must be the instigator of getting people together. Again, this is where your calendar plays an important role. Planning ahead to meet with people where you can have quality time and deeper conversations is imperative to moving relationships deeper. Time goes by so quickly, we are so busy, that if we don't plan our time, we will never get around to spending time with lost people.

A hard reality about investing in lostness is that it also means that you will have to limit your time with other Christians. I'm not suggesting that you cut out Christian fellowship, but in order to bring new people into your life, it means that you will have less time to spend with other Christians. They key is to have balance in your life. You need to make sure that you have sufficient Christian fellowship that is needed in your walk with the Lord, but you also need to have space in your life to welcome new people.

Once you have created space in your life to receive new people, how do you incorporate them into your life? There are several ways to get people involved in your life:

1. Sharing Meals Together

This is a topic that has already been touched on but is worth revisiting. One of the greatest ways to build relationships is to do it over meals. There is something about food that brings people together. One, meals are times where people slow down for a minute. Two, everyone has to eat. Three, people associate food with fellowship. You can meet people at restaurants, have them over to your home for a meal, or pack a picnic and meet people at the park or the ballfield.

2. Inviting People into Your Home

You really get to know people when you visit them in their homes. This seems to be becoming rarer and rarer in our culture. With the busyness of life, people seem to not use their homes to host people like they used to do. When you invite someone into your home, you are inviting him into your life in a deeper way than when you simply meet people outside the home.

3. Sharing the Ups and Downs of Life

Life is a series of mountain tops and valleys. We all have moments of great celebration and times of great sorrow. As you get to know people and are trying to develop deeper relationships, try and take advantage of the ups and downs of life. Learning to truly celebrate with people when they have mountain top experiences can open the door for the Gospel. Showing up to the weekly game with a birthday cake to celebrate someone's birthday goes so much further than simply saying Happy Birthday. Organizing a baby shower or diaper drive for expecting parents shows that you really care. Taking a friend out to dinner to celebrate her promotion at work is so much more meaningful than simply saying congratulations. People feel valued when they are celebrated. Celebrating the wins in people's lives will draw you into deeper relationships with them.

While celebrating wins is important to building deeper relationships with people, being there for folks when times are tough is even more important. So called friends are easy to find when things are good, but true friends show-up when things get bad. Seek to be the true friend. When someone is in the hospital, stop by and visit and bring a care package. See if he needs help getting his kids to school or activities. When someone loses his job, look for ways to practically help him and his family. When someone loses a family member, drop off food. I've had multiple people lament over how many of their friends did not offer any assistance during difficult times in their lives. It is during these difficult times that you can show the love and compassion of God. Furthermore, your actions will give you a great platform to speak truth into your friend's life.

4. Share Burdens

Sharing common burdens can help you build deeper relationships. Offer to watch people's children so the parents can have a date night. Take turns getting kids to events. Be available to take someone to a doctor's appointment. Drop off a meal if you know someone is having a busy week. These are all examples on how you can share the day-to-day burdens that people face.

Chapter 10
Moving Conversations to Spiritual Issues

It is easy to talk about sports, kids' activities, family issues, and other day-to-day topics. You, however, might find it difficult to move towards spiritual conversations. One critique about a more relational style evangelism as compared to drive-by witnessing, is that people never get to the Gospel. This can be a real challenge. How do you move from casual conversations to spiritual conversations? Here are some tips.

1. Ask about people's foundation for their beliefs.

I have found that many people have never really considered the foundation for what they believe. For example, most lost people, unless they are part of a world religion, practice what I call imaginary friendism. You may be wondering what in the world imaginary friendism is. Let me tell you. It is not uncommon for a child to have an imaginary friend. That imaginary friend likes to do what the child likes to do. The imaginary friend thinks the way the kid thinks. The imaginary friend approves of what the kid approves. When that kid grows up, his imaginary friend often becomes his god. When you ask someone what he believes about God, he typically believes in a god that thinks the way he thinks, acts the way he wants him to act, and approves what he approves. Basically, his imaginary friend has become his god. When you ask that person why he believes what he believes, he cannot point to any authoritative source. It is simply what he thinks. There is no difference between the imaginary friend he had as a child and the god in which he now believes.

By challenging people on the foundation for what they believe, it opens the door for you to share the foundation for what you believe. You can share with them the biblical worldview on the various issues that you are discussing. This can easily lead to the Gospel.

2. Focus on the Solutions the Bible Gives to Everyday Living

I think Christians are often known for what they are against as opposed to what they are for. For instance, Christians are known (or at least used to be known) for being against divorce. But are Christians known for believing that you can have a wonderful, fulfilling marriage? Do unbelievers know the Biblical principles that lead to having such a marriage? Sometimes Christians are quick to point out what is wrong, without taking the time to show what is right, good, and fulfilling. When people are having problems with their children, showing them that the Bible gives a lot of wise counsel in how to rear children can open people to wanting to know more about what the Bible says. The Bible has so much to say about how to live a good life, but we sometimes focus only on what the Bible says not to do. We shouldn't hesitate from talking about sin, but it should springboard into a discussion about what we should do. Here are some more examples:

- You're talking with a man who is frustrated with his wife. He tells you everything that she doesn't do that he wants her to do. Or he is explaining all of the things that she does that he absolutely hates. He is so frustrated that he is considering divorce. You could take him to Ephesians 5 and talk about what the Bible says a husband should do. Paul tells the church in Ephesus that husbands should love their wives like Christ loved the church. How did Jesus show love to the church? He sacrificed for the church, he ministered to the church, he was even willing to do tasks such as washing the disciples' feet. Challenge your friend to stop focusing on what his wife is doing or not doing and seek to be the husband that God has called him to be. How is he loving his wife? What does he do that makes her feel unloved. How is he sacrificing for his wife. The verse also says that he is to cherish his wife. What is he doing that shows she is really cherished? We can't control what other people do, but we can control what we do. If he will focus on being the husband that God has called him to be, he may see that his wife has a softening of her heart and starts to respond in a more positive way.

- Another friend is struggling with his preteen son. He constantly forgets things that he needs for school or practice. He can never get his stuff together. He is just not showing any sort of responsibility. The Bible says that fathers are to bring their sons up in the discipline and instruction of the Lord. That word discipline does not simply mean punishment. It is a word that is used to train horses. Part of training a horse is to put practices in place that help develop the behavior the trainer wants the horse to exhibit. What processes can the father implement that will help his son be more responsible? Maybe he needs to put a clipboard by the front door that has a list of everything his son needs for school. Each morning, before he and his son leave the house, they start a practice of stopping at the door and going through the list. Then the son progresses to where he checks the list himself. This is utilizing processes that will help train him to check to ensure he has everything he needs.

- A third friend believes his teenage daughter has friends who are really a bad influence. He is worried about the path she is taking because of this bad influence. The Bible has a lot to say about peer pressure. God has created us to need fellowship with other people. We must be careful about who fulfills this need because they can put pressure on us to act in certain ways. The key is finding a group that will put good peer pressure on you. Instead of just saying she can't hang out with her friends, which is wise, work on helping her find a new place to meet that fellowship need. Maybe getting involved with a local church youth program will help her find friends that will have a positive impact.

- Maybe you know a young person that is frustrated that he is not getting promoted at work. You know from your conversations with him that he has struggled with being on time and with attention to details. You share with him that the Bible teaches that before you entrust someone with a big responsibility, he should prove himself with a little responsibility. Help him develop a plan that addresses the areas where he is not proving trustworthy. As he proves himself to his boss, he will probably be rewarded with greater responsibility and position.

These are just a few examples of how the Bible gives practical wisdom in how to live and thrive. While the Bible does speak to theological issues, it also speaks to day-to-day living. Showing people this can open their hearts to the Word, which can quickly lead to Gospel conversations. There is an old saying that some people are so heavenly minded that they are of no earthly good. While the Bible is very much heavenly minded, it is also very good for instructing us in how to practically live our lives.

3. Focus on the Philippians 4:8 list in Your Conversations

Philippians 4:8 says: "Finally, brothers, whatever is true, whatever is honorable, whatever is just, whatever is pure, whatever is lovely, whatever is commendable, if there is any excellence, if there is anything worthy of praise, think about these things." We live in a culture that loves everything opposite of this list. We see this in how popular so many reality shows are that focus on drama, backbiting, gossip, and the tearing down of people. Let your speech focus on the things Paul instructed us to think about. People are drawn to other people who are uplifting. Be that person.

4. Be a Safe Person

How you say something can be as important as what you say. Sometimes people are offended by what we say, not because of the truth, but because of how we deliver the truth. If we are harsh, reactionary, or come across as self-righteous, then we can turn people off to the truth. As people realize that you are a Christian, you may find that they try to test you. They may say things that they know you will not agree with. Sometimes they do this to see how you will react. It is important that they realize that you always try to speak with grace and compassion. They need to know that you will say what you believe is true, but that you will do it in a kind and gentle way. In my cigar Bible study, I have worked hard to create an environment where people feel safe to ask any question they might have. They will not be talked down to, or ridiculed, or admonished because of their question. They will be answered in a calm, measured, loving way. Sometimes the truth is hard, but that does not mean I have to present it in a hard manner. I'm reminded of what Paul said in 1 Corinthians 13:1-2: "If I speak in the tongues of men and of angels, but have not love, I am a noisy gong or a clanging cymbal. [2] And if I have prophetic powers, and understand all mysteries and all knowledge, and if I have all faith, so as to remove mountains, but have not love, I am nothing." I may have all the answers, but if I do not share in a spirit of love, then I am but a clanging cymbal.

Another important aspect of being a safe person is that people know that you are a person that shows proper discretion. You are not going to gossip about them. You are not going to blab to others the struggles they have shared with you. They need to know that you can control your tongue. With that said, when someone says I want to tell you something, but you must promise not to tell anyone, I never agree to that. There are some things that must be reported. If someone is abusing a child, I have a legal and ethical obligation to report it. If someone is suicidal, I have an obligation to make sure he receives the help that he needs. What I do promise, is that I will not gossip about anything they share with me and that I will handle it with appropriate discretion.

5. Pray with People

We have spent time examining the need to pray for people, but it is also important to pray with people. As I previously shared, telling people that you pray for them often can open their hearts to the Gospel. As powerful as that is, actually praying with someone can be more powerful. Sometimes people may feel uncomfortable at first when you are praying with them, but if you get the opportunity to, it often impacts them in a profound way. Your prayer doesn't have to be elegant or lengthy. Sometimes you will pray for God to intervein. Sometimes you will pray for God to comfort their hearts. Sometimes you will pray for God to give them clarity on a decision.

When you have finished praying with the person, make a commitment that you will continue praying for him. If you make that commitment, be sure to follow through with it. Be faithful to continue praying and take opportunities to follow-up with the person to see what God is doing.

6. Share the Gospel

The entire point of developing first, second, and third space ministry is to share the Gospel. As I have given you different strategies on how to move the conversation to spiritual things, I also want to encourage you to share the Gospel. As you utilize these strategies, take the opportunity to discuss the root issue – their relationship with God. As you are talking with people through different issues they are facing, ask them: "What does your relationship with God look like?" That question can be followed up with: "How does a person have a relationship with God?" From there, you can move into a Gospel witness.

I want to emphasize again that you do not have to spend a long time building a relationship with someone before you share the Gospel. The goal of these different strategies is to lead you to a Gospel conversation. Sometimes you may get to share the Gospel early on in a relationship, but the person does not accept Jesus as his Lord and Savior. A statistic that has been thrown around for years is that the average person hears the Gospel seven times before he is saved. I'm not sure how accurate that is, but there is Biblical evidence that people often have to hear multiple times before they are saved. In 1 Corinthians 3:6, Paul states: "I planted, Apollos watered, but God gave the growth." While this verse may be referring to the fact that Paul led people to the Lord and then Apollos helped them grow in their faith, I do not think it is unreasonable to believe that it also means that for some they first heard the Gospel from Paul, but then also from Apollos before they believed. Furthermore, the Bible speaks about God's patience in withholding judgement so that people have time to repent. Knowing this, you want to freely share the Gospel in a way that you continue to have more opportunities in the future in case they do not receive it the first time. You want to approach the Gospel through a natural conversation, which is different than a drive-by witness.

Chapter 11
Secondary Opportunity

It is worth noting that while your main purpose for developing ministry in your first, second, or third space, is to reach lost people, you will come across people who are already believers but are not really walking with the Lord. Some of them may be marginally involved with a local church, but some may not be in Christian fellowship at all. While these folks are not your primary target, you can have an opportunity to help them start walking with the Lord and living out their faith in the context of community.

As you encounter Christians who are not walking with the Lord, let me encourage you to do the following:

1. Confirm Their Salvation

Just because someone says he is a Christian; doesn't mean he is one. I would have told you that I was a Christian before I understood salvation. I went to a Christian church, attended Sunday School, had been baptized, and was active in the life of a local church. The problem is that I was lost. When we meet people in our ministry areas that say they are Christian, we should engage them in conversation about what it means to be saved and how to be saved.

2. Seek to Get Them in the Word

When we meet a believer who is not involved in church, we usually start inviting him to be a part of ours. I have found that before I start pressing someone to come to church, that I have greater success if I can first get them in the Word. As I build a relationship with a person, I want to help him understand the importance of being in the Word daily, or at least regularly. The more that he gets into the Word, the more you will begin to see his life change.

The question becomes, how do you get people interested in the Word? First, if they are really saved, I believe the Holy Spirit will begin to lead them to the Word as they have someone invest in them through a discipling relationship. Second, as you have the same type of conversations detailed earlier – conversations that point people to the practical wisdom of the Bible, that will begin to wet their appetite for the Word. Third, I believe there is great power in praying for them to develop a love for the Word. Forth, you can invite them to start a reading plan with you. Sometimes people just need someone who will come alongside them and walk with them. Be sure that you do not pick a reading plan that is too challenging. I'd rather have them be consistent reading the Word for ten minutes, five times a week, than try to get them to read an hour a day, knowing that it will be overwhelming, and they will probably fail. Set realistic goals for them.

3. Invite Them to Be a Part of Your Ministry

As they see you engaging people with the Gospel, they will be challenged in their faith. Inviting them to be a part of what you are doing can help them get moving in their walk with the Lord. An easy way to get them involved is to invite them to pray for those in the group who are lost.

4. Seek to Get Them Involved in a Local Church

The Bible knows nothing of a believer who refuses to be actively involved in a local church. God has called us to live out our faith amid Christian community. As you challenge the person to get in the Word, and as God begins working in his heart, you should see a greater desire for obedience. Use the Word to show him how important the local church is, and how being a part of it is required to walk in obedience.

While seeking to win lost people to Jesus through my third-space ministry, I have seen a number of believers who were not walking with the Lord begin to grow in their relationship and obedience to Jesus. Some of them have become strong partners in ministry and have seen their lives and their families transformed because of their renewed walk with the Lord. Some of them were just never discipled. Some moved to Las Vegas and just never got involved with a church. Whatever the reason they grew distant from the Lord, it has been a joy to be a part of their journey back into close fellowship with Jesus and His church. Some of them have ended up at my church, some have ended up at other churches. I rejoice in both, as long as they are walking with the Lord and involved in a Bible believing church.

Chapter 12
Closing Exhortation

My hope for this book is that it has given you two things. First, practical training that helps equip you to live out your calling as a witness. The second, a greater passion for witnessing. With that said, I want to close with examining two passages to help stroke the fires of evangelism within you. The first passage is Romans 10:13-15: "For 'everyone who calls on the name of the Lord will be saved.' [14] How then will they call on him in whom they have not believed? And how are they to believe in him of whom they have never heard? And how are they to hear without someone preaching? [15] And how are they to preach unless they are sent? As it is written, 'How beautiful are the feet of those who preach the good news!'"

This passage begins with the clearest statement on how one is saved – by calling on the name of the Lord. It is a picture of someone who realizes he is in desperate need and calls out for help. Lost people are indeed in desperate need. They are separated from God because of their sin. They stand guilty before a Holy God, who will bring judgement for sin. They also stand, however, before a God who is compassionate and quick to save. This verse also shows that the Gospel is open to anyone who will call upon Jesus. It doesn't matter your background, economic status, family, or ethnicity – the Gospel is open to anyone who will call out for help. It also emphasizes who you are calling upon. You don't just call upon a good teacher, or a guru, or a prophet. You call upon the LORD Jesus. You recognize Him for who He is – the Lord.

After Paul, the writer of Romans, states how to be saved, he then asks a question: "How will they call on him in whom they have not believed?" Why do people not believe in Jesus? For some, they do not believe because they want to live their lives their own way. They do not want to recognize and submit to a lord. The basis of their unbelief is a rebellious heart. For others, they do not believe because they have been deceived by false teaching. They have been taught to believe in someone or something else. This verse, however, address another reason why some people do not believe – it is because they have not heard the Gospel. "And how are they to believe in him of whom they have never heard?" A person can't believe in something or someone he has never heard of. But why have they not heard? Paul addresses this when he says: "And how are they to hear without someone preaching?" The reason they have never heard is because they have never been told. The word preaching does not necessarily mean a pastor, but rather a proclaimer. People haven't heard because no one has been willing to proclaim the Gospel to them.

I think it is easy for those of us who live in the United States to believe that everyone has heard. This is, after all, a "Christian nation." This belief is a false belief. So many people have never had anyone simply explain the Gospel to them. This is illustrated in the story I shared earlier about the college guys that went out on a campus in the middle of the Bible belt and found that most of the students they talked to had not heard the Gospel. No wonder they were not saved. How could they be? How could they believe in something they had never heard? My prayer for you as the reader is that you will begin to look at people differently. My prayer is that every person you know, and every person you encounter, you will begin to ask yourself the question: "Have they heard the Gospel?" We must repent of assuming that someone else will tell lost people how to be saved. We must answer the call of Jesus to be his witnesses.

The second verse that I want to examine in this closing section is Romans 1:16: "For I am not ashamed of the gospel, for it is the power of God for salvation to everyone who believes, to the Jew first and also to the Greek." Paul begins this verse by stating that he is not ashamed of the Gospel. Far too many times in my life I could not make this statement. There have been times I have been ashamed of the Gospel. I was afraid people would think less of me because I am a Christian. I was afraid that people might find the message of the Gospel foolishness. Maybe they would make fun of me for trying to witness to them. Paul, however, was not ashamed of the Gospel. Are you ashamed of the Gospel? How does your life reveal the answer to that question? If you do not share the Gospel on a regular basis, is it maybe because you find yourself ashamed of the Gospel? If so, ask the Lord to change your heart and give you confidence in the Gospel.

Paul then tells us why he is not ashamed of the Gospel – it is the power of God for salvation. I have been asked many times if I believe aliens exist in space. My answer has always been that I do not believe there are aliens. I had a person once ask me, "If there are no aliens in space, then why did God go through all of the work of creating so many galaxies and planets?" Instead of going into a longer explanation about how the Bible teaches the heavens declare the glory of God, I simply responded with the question: "What work?" The book of Genesis declares that God spoke creation into existence. That is how powerful God is – that He could simply speak, and everything came into existence. This very power is unleashed for salvation when you share the Gospel. This means that not only has God promised to empower you as we discussed earlier, but that He has also given us the Gospel, which unleashes His very power to save people. We should have great confidence in the Gospel because it is powerful and changes people's lives.

One more note on this passage is that Paul tells us that the Gospel is the power of God for salvation to everyone who believes. He then emphasizes this by stating: "to the Jew first, and also to the Greek." Paul is saying that this Gospel is for everyone. It is so easy for us to believe that a certain person you know would not be interested. It is so easy to think that a person could never be saved. We can think that someone is too successful to care about the Gospel. We think another person is too involved in a different religion to be saved. We think that a person is too sinful to want to hear about Jesus. This verse tells us that the Gospel should be shared with everyone. What is particularly encouraging about this verse is the fact that it was written by a guy that most people thought would never accept Jesus. Paul was a persecutor of the church before he was saved. He was on his way to imprison Christians when he encountered Jesus. If Paul could be saved, anyone can be saved.

Whether you are at the beginning of your witnessing journey, or are continuing what you have already been doing, I hope these verses will serve to remind you of the need for people to hear the Gospel and the power that is unleashed when you share the Good News of Jesus Christ. That does not mean that everyone you witness to will be saved, but you will have done your part in that person's life to ensure that he had the opportunity to believe because he had an opportunity to hear.

Finally, let me encourage you to take action. The book of James tells us that we are not just to be hearers of the Word, but doers of the Word. Let me encourage you to use the form below to write down action steps that can help you move forward with developing first, second, or third space ministry.

Action Steps

Now that you have finished this book, the question you should answer is: "What next steps must I take to move forward?" Use this form to set goals to begin living a missional life.

1. **What area of my life do I want to begin focusing on for evangelism? (circle one)**

   a. Where I live

   b. Where I work

   c. Where I play

2. **What are the three to five steps that I need to do to begin engaging the above area missionally?**

   a._____

   b._____

   c._____

   d._____

   e._____

3. Assign dates for the above steps:

a._____

b._____

c._____

d._____

e._____

4. Who will you recruit to be your accountability partner to help encourage you to follow through with the above? Set a deadline for asking him or her to serve in this role.

a._____

Appendix A
Quick Guide Strategies

This appendix is to help give you a quick guide on how to move forward with different ministry opportunities. I will give two examples from the first and third spaces (where you live and where you play). Even if you are not using these exact activities, you can use these strategies as a template to build your own.

First Space Strategies

Block Party

Hosting a block party at your house is a great way to start the process of getting to know your neighbors and developing community within your neighborhood. Here are steps to take for your block party:

1. **Calendar the Event** – Make sure you give enough time to prepare for the party. Try to avoid holiday weekends. Choose a day that works for the demographic of the neighborhood. For example, a weeknight may work in an older community, but you will need to pick the weekend for a younger demographic.

2. **Prayer Walk Your Neighborhood** – Take a few weeks and prayer walk your neighborhood each night. Pray for each house. Pray for the families. Pray that God would give you favor with your neighbors. Ask God to show you where He is working.

3. **Pass Out Invitations** – Two weeks before the event, pass out invitations by going door-to-door in your neighborhood. Be sure to include all the pertinent information that they need – date, time, address, and any other information. Do they need to bring anything? Is there a theme? Will there be drinks and food?

4. **Prepare Invitations for a Second Event** – plan a second block party a few months later. Have invitations for it ready to hand out at the first

block party. You are trying to build momentum and relationships – this does not happen with only one event.

5. **Host the Party** – Try to create an environment that helps people to get to know each other. This can be done through nametags, games that help people get to know each other, and seating that puts people in groups.

6. **Exchange Numbers** – Try to exchange numbers with at least three new neighbors. This way you can start communicating with people.

7. **Set a meal appointment** – Try to set at least one follow-up lunch or dinner appointment with a neighbor that you don't know well.

8. **Pass out Invitations** – Be sure to pass out the invitations for the second block party.

Book Club

A book club is a great way to bring people together for fellowship around an activity that many people enjoy – reading. Here are some steps to launching and using a book club for ministry.

1. **Weekly or Monthly** – Most book clubs meet monthly, but some meet more often. Typically, a monthly meeting has the assumption that people will have read the book before you meet. You can, however, meet more often, and discuss the book as you read through it. For example, you could meet weekly to discuss three chapters. The more times you meet the more opportunity you have to build relationships. Think through who you are targeting for your club and plan accordingly. Busy moms may not be able to meet once a week. They might, however, be able to meet twice a month.

2. **Calendar the Launch** – Choose a launch date for your club and for the meetings. Try to create enough space in your calendar for time before and after the meeting. That is a great way to get more out of the meeting by having time to invite some of the folks to show up early for fellowship, or you are not pushed to move on to your next appointment in the event that good discussion is happening following the meeting.

3. **Pick the First Book** – The first book you read as a group is a strategic decision. If you have people that you think are interested in spiritual things, then you may pick a religious book. If, however, you have people that would probably not attend if they thought it is a religious book club, then pick a secular book. Also, it can be a club that exclusively reads fiction or one that reads non-fiction.

4. **Invite People** – There are many ways to invite people. You can send invite cards, text message people, send invites online, or by personally asking someone to be a part of the group. You can also let other people invite folks they think would like to join.

5. **Pray** – Pray daily for the people who are going to be a part of the group. As you get to know the members you can let them know that you pray for them daily and that they are welcome to share requests if they ever have specific things they would like you to pray about.

6. **Prepare Questions** – An important aspect of a good book club is good discussion. This is facilitated by having prepared questions. There are many resources online that can help you develop a list of questions. An example is bookclubs.com that has a lot of resources for starting and leading a book club.

7. **Kick-off Meeting** – Host your first meeting. Be sure to create a welcoming environment. Have nametags and give people an opportunity to introduce themselves. Have them share a little bit about themselves. Create a group text so that you can communicate with everyone in the group.

8. **Reminder Texts** – Each week, the day before or the day of the meeting send out a reminder text about the meeting. Include what reading you are going to cover.

9. **Outside Meetings** – As you get moving with the group, look for opportunities to have meetings with members of the group. Share a meal together. Plan a play date for the kids. Just look for ways to connect outside of the group.

10. **Season Your Words with Grace** – As you discuss the books, look for ways to incorporate your faith into the discussion. This can lead to Gospel conversations.

Third Space Strategies

Children's Sports Team

Utilizing your children's activities to engage other families with the Gospel is often an overlooked mission field. Here is a strategy for witnessing during your child's sports season.

1. **Calendar the Season** – As your child's sports season begins, be sure to pull out your calendar and look at when you will have practices and games. Schedule your calendar so that you have time to invite people to do dinner after practice or other such activities.

2. **Pray for the families** – You and your children begin praying for the other children on the team and their families. Ask God to give you favor with them and to show you which families you should begin engaging in relationship. This is also a great opportunity to develop a family devotional time. Spend time in the Word and prayer. As part of your prayer time, pray for the families on your child's team. As the parent, ask the other parents how you can be praying for them during your family devotional time. Teach your kids to ask their teammates the same question.

3. **Engage families** – Begin seeking to connect with different families on the team. Share meals together after games and practices. Invite them to go to the park on a Saturday. Have them over to the house for a BBQ. Be intentional with the relationships you form with those on your child's team.

4. **Share the Gospel** – As you have opportunities, share the Gospel.

Hiking Club

Hiking can provide a great third space ministry platform. Here is a strategy for getting started.

1. **Join or Start?** – At the beginning you need to decide if you want to try and start your own hiking club or join an existing one. There are several factors to consider when making this decision. First, you need to see what preexisting groups exist in your area. You can do a search on the web or go to websites such as meetup.com to find group hikes in your area. There may not be an official group to join, but that the same people lead hikes on a regular basis. Second, if you want to start your own, do you have enough contacts who would be committed to hiking? Third, what level of knowledge do you have of hiking? In some areas, little previous knowledge is needed. In other areas, such as areas with extreme temperatures or elevation changes, having experience is prudent before leading others. Personally, I would first seek to join a group and try that before I would ever start my own.

2. **Calendar Dates** – Make sure you calendar the dates of the hikes and protect that time. Try to add space to meet up with people before and after the hike.

3. **Start Hiking** – Sometimes it is hard for people to start a new activity, especially if they do not know anyone else. Don't procrastinate in getting started, just jump in and start joining the group hikes.

4. **Remember Names** – Personally, I am bad with names. However, in my third space ministry, I try hard to learn people's names. It really connects you with someone when you see him a second time and you can call him by name.

5. **Pray for People** – As you start to get to know the people in the group, start building a prayer list of people you pray for every day. As you have opportunity, let them know that you pray for them regularly.

6. **Outside Meetings** – Seek to connect with people outside of the hikes. For example, see if any of the hikers would like to grab a meal after the hike. You could even pack a picnic and bring some camping chairs for you to sit around and eat after the hike if they don't want to go to a restaurant. Look for opportunities to connect with each other's families.

7. **Be a Friend** – As you get to know people it is important that you be a friend to them. That means you celebrate wins with them. If it is their

birthday, get them something or take them to lunch. If they are going through a difficult time, then offer to help. Some people struggle with moving from acquaintance to friend because they never start acting like a friend.

8. **Season Your Words with Grace** – Remember to talk freely about your faith in a way that doesn't come across as if you are preaching to them, but that they see you have a real relationship with God. Also, when discussing weighty issues, point them to what the Word of God says about the subject.

9. **Share the Gospel** – Take every opportunity you have to share the Gospel. You don't have to wait months to be able to start sharing but let me also caution you against coming across as if the only reason you are there is to try and convert people.

Appendix B
Strategies for Witnessing to Specific People

Strategy for Witnessing to Family

It is natural for believers to want their family members to be saved. Many, however, struggle with how to share the Gospel with them. Witnessing to family can be one of the greatest challenges for several reasons. Your family usually knows you better than anyone else. They know your weaknesses and failures. Another challenge is that you want to maintain a good relationship with your family members. Sometimes Christians are afraid that their family members will get angry with them if they try to talk to them about Jesus. This is especially true if your family members are very hostile to spiritual things. Because of this, you want to share in a way that preserves family relationships as much as possible.

Here is a five-step strategy for witnessing to your family members. I hope it will help you overcome any barriers you have with sharing the Good News with them.

1. Live

Living an authentic Christian life creates the greatest platform for evangelism. This is especially true for those who know you best. Be sure that your Christian walk is not simply church attendance, but rather, let your family see that your relationship with Jesus is the most important thing in your life. Your daily quiet time, your church involvement, Holy living, and your joyful service all work to develop your platform from which to share. Remind them often that you are not worthy of Heaven in your own righteousness, but you are grateful that God is a God of grace.

2. Pray

It is crucial that you are faithful to pray for lost family members. You want to pray for the following:

1. A softening of the heart

    a. Pray that God would tear down any barriers to the Gospel and would soften your family member's heart.

2. Wisdom

    a. Ask God to give you wisdom to know when to speak and when not to speak.

3. Opportunity

    a. Ask God to give you divine opportunities to speak truth into your family member's life. Use language that is 'seasoned with grace'.

4. Partners

    a. Ask God to send people into the life of your family member who will share the Gospel.

3. Speak

As God gives you opportunities, speak truth into the life of your family member. Don't just speak about Jesus when you are trying to convert someone, but rather season your words with grace at all times. Be sensitive to know if you are pushing an issue, or if God has opened the door for you. Also, we often are more reactionary with family members than we are with more casual acquaintances. Do not respond in anger or become frustrated during Gospel conversations with your family members. Try to create an environment where it is safe for them to ask questions and even challenge what you believe.

4. Love

You have the opportunity to show love to your lost family member. This does not mean you enable sin, but you can always show unconditional love. Look for ways to minister and show this love in a tangible way.

5. Ambush

Be intentional about sending people to your lost family members to witness to them. Ambush them as often as you can. If you know of other believers in their lives speak to them about the importance of sharing the Gospel with your family member. Call a local church in their area and ask them to make a witnessing visit.

You may want to ask them to not mention you sent them as that may not be well received by your family member.

Strategy for Witnessing to a Religious Person
John 3:1-3, 16

I have often encountered people who were trusting in their religious works to be saved. When the issue of Heaven comes up, these folks will start talking about what religion they are affiliated with or how faithful they are in their religion. They will also point to different religious rituals, such as baptism, that they have completed. When I think about these people, I think about what Jesus said in Matthew 7:21: "Not everyone who says to me, 'Lord, Lord,' will enter the kingdom of heaven, but the one who does the will of my Father who is in heaven.[3] This passage scares a lot of people because they wonder how can anyone be certain he or she is going to Heaven? What is Jesus talking about? The issue becomes evident in the next few verses. Jesus gives the people's responses. The argument they start giving as to why they should go to Heaven isn't centered on what Christ did on the cross, but rather on their own religious works. Did we not prophecy in your name? Did we not cast out demons in your name? Did we not do mighty works in your name? All these responses show that they were not trusting in Jesus's work on the cross, but rather, on their own religious works. They believed Jesus should let them into Heaven because of all of the great ministry they did in His name.

The Gospel of John, chapter three is a great passage to share with someone who is trusting in religious works. Let's look at this passage.

1. Nicodemus

The Bibles tells us three things about Nicodemus.

> a. He was a Pharisee. This meant that he was a member of the elite religious group of his day. One of the requirements to become a Pharisee was to memorize the first five books of the Old Testament and recite them seven times without error.

---

[3] *The Holy Bible: English Standard Version* (Wheaton, IL: Crossway Bibles, 2016), Mt 7:21.

b. He was a ruler. Nicodemus was a man of high position. He was a man that people listened to, a man that people respected. He was not a person of low moral character. He had power and influence.

c. He was a Jew. Because he was a ruler of the Jews, as well as a Pharisee, we know that he was a Jew himself. This meant that he was from the right racial background. He was a part of the chosen people of God.

2. Jesus' statement

Jesus makes a very profound statement in verse three. He tells Nicodemus that if he wants to see Heaven, he must be born again. This statement does three things:

a. It points the conversation to an issue of eternity. We need to be concerned about issues of eternity.

b. It separates salvation from works.

c. It strips away all that Nicodemus was trusting in for salvation. Nicodemus was trusting in his religious affiliation, his zealous devotion, and his racial heritage.

3. Jesus' Gives Clarity

Jesus sheds light on what he meant by being born again. In verse sixteen, he shows Nicodemus, and all of us, how to be saved. This verse shows us three things:

a. That salvation is available to us because God loves us. It was love for us, sinners, that motivated God to send His only Son, Jesus Christ. Even though we had turned against God by sinning against Him, He still showed love to us.

b. That salvation is provided through Jesus' works and not ours. Jesus came to die for our sins. He came to take the punishment for our sins. No matter how religious we might be, it still took Jesus to bridge the gap that sin puts between God and us.

c. That which we are trusting in for salvation must move from trusting in ourselves, to trusting in what Jesus did for us – he paid the price for our sins! The word "believe," does not mean head knowledge, but could be translated: "trust." Whoever trusts in Jesus will not perish but have everlasting life.

4. Conclusion

From this text we see that even the most religious of people still needs Jesus. They still need to be "born again," which happens by trusting in Jesus. The wonderful thing about the use of the term, "born again," is that we can learn two major things from it:

> a. That it happens at a particular point in time. When a baby is born in America, they receive a birth certificate. It tells the exact date and time the baby was born. Some people believe that salvation is a process that lasts a long time. While the Holy Spirit may draw some people for years, true conversion takes place at a particular moment in time. Salvation is not a process - it is an event.

> b. A birth is not the end, but the beginning of something new. When a person gets saved, that is not the end. When a person is born again, they begin a new and wonderful life as a child of God. This life, which they have now been given, will not pass away (even though this fleshly body might), but it will last for eternity.

5. A final question

What are you trusting in, religious works, or Jesus' death on the cross for your sins? Have you ever been born again? Has there ever been a time where you took your trust for salvation off of you and placed it in Jesus Christ?

- ## Philippians 3:4-11

Philippians 3:4-11 is a great place to witness to a religious person. Paul gives his testimony about going from trusting in his religious credentials and accomplishments to trusting in Jesus Christ alone. Paul is arguing that if anyone could get to Heaven based on good works and being religious, he should have more confidence than anyone else. He had impressive spiritual credentials:

- He had been through the right religious rituals.

- He was from the right nation.

- He was from the right family.

- He was the right race.

- He was part of the right religious group.

- He was zealous.

- He was more faithful than anyone he knew.

Though Paul had this list of credentials that he thought would get him into Heaven, he came to realize that he had to let go of all of them to gain Christ. He had to stop trusting in what he was doing and put his faith solely in what Jesus had done for him on the cross. He found true righteousness – not that comes from the law but comes through faith in Jesus.

Strategy for Witnessing to Someone Who is Part of a Cult or World Religion

1. **Ask the person to share what he/she believes and why he/she believes it.**

   a. Listen with great intensity. Sometimes we ask questions, but we are not really interested in how people answer it. Have you ever been in a discussion with someone, and you find yourself not really listening to the person because you are too busy formulating what you are going to say? Using active listening techniques, such as nodding your head, making eye contact, and leaning in are ways to show that you are interested in what the person is saying. It is also a good practice to ask clarifying questions to make sure you understand what they are saying. Remind yourself that you should care about the person, not just about winning the debate.

   b. Do not interrupt. It is easy when someone is telling us what he believes, and he says something we do not agree with, to interrupt. We can then get drawn into a debate or argument, which is not the goal of the conversation.

2. **Share with the person what you believe and why you believe it.**

   a. Share the Gospel just like you would with anyone else. If the person interrupts, remind him that you listened to him and therefore he should let you share what you believe before you begin discussing it.

b. Give the person an opportunity to receive Jesus as Lord and Savior. This way when the person leaves you know he has had an opportunity to receive Jesus. Also, it helps you ensure that he knows how to be saved. It is easy to start debating different points of disagreement and never get to the Gospel. You may even win the debate, but you have actually lost if they never got to hear how to be saved.

3. Challenge what they believe.

a. Once you have clearly shared the Gospel, then go back and start challenging what their religion teaches. I have found it helpful to use primary documents when possible. For example, if I am speaking to a Mormon, I don't want to pull out my Anti-Mormon evangelism book and refer to that. I want to pull out their own documents and quote directly from them. I did this once with two Mormon missionaries. You should have seen their eyes when I pulled out The Journal of Discourse and read directly from their authorized book.

4. Remember their cost.

a. One of the things to remember about someone who is part of a world religion or cult is that his ties to that religion are much more than theological. Most Muslims are Muslim because of community more than conviction. This is clear when you see that most of them do not pray five times a day, or go to the mosque, or keep the fast during Ramadan. True conviction would lead to adherence to the faith. That is not to say they lack any belief, but rather, it is the connection with the community that binds them to the religion more than the theological teachings. Understanding this is important because the cost of them walking away from their religion can be high. If a secular person, whose family is not really involved in a faith system, gets saved, the chances of him facing a lot of persecution is much smaller than say, a Muslim, who leaves Islam. The Muslim man could lose his family, his job, all of his friends, face physical persecution, and even death. Depending on where he lives, he could also face legal issues and be thrown in jail. While Jesus is worth losing everything for, we should be sensitive to people who are wrestling with that decision. We should also be willing to help people deal with the consequences of following Jesus.

Strategy for Someone Who Believes There is No Hope for Them to be Saved

The overwhelming majority of people that I witness to think or at least hope they are going to Heaven. Occasionally, I will run across someone who things there is no hope for him to be saved. This is usually because the person feels he has done something so horrible that he cannot be saved. One thing to remember when dealing with someone like this, is that the person is still trusting in a works-based salvation. He believes going to Heaven is based on works; he just believes he has done too many bad things to ever warrant him going to Heaven.

1. Ask the person: "What do you think is the worst sin a person could ever commit?" The typical answers I usually receive to this question are murder or abusing a child.

2. Respond by saying: "While those are horrible sins, I think the worst sin that someone could ever commit would be to have actually murder Jesus. It is bad enough if you murder a regular person, but to have murdered Jesus, I don't there is a worse sin that could be committed. Do you think that person could be saved?"

3. The Bible tells us how Jesus responded to the people murdering Him. Luke 23:34 states: "And Jesus said, "Father, forgive them, for they know not what they do"

4. You see, Jesus was willing to offer forgiveness even to the men that tortured and killed Him. It doesn't matter what you have done, Jesus offers forgiveness because that forgiveness is based on what He did for us, not on our actions. The reality is that we are all deserving of Hell.

5. I believe that you feel you have no hope to go to Heaven because you believe going to Heaven is based on a set of scales and that your bad outweighs your good. The Bible does not present going to Heaven as based on a set of scales where you good is weighed against your bad, but rather on a law. The question is whether or not you have broken God's law. The Bible teaches that all of us have broken God's law.

6. At this point, move to sharing the same scriptures you would with anyone else. Romans 3:10, Romans 3:23, Romans 6:23a, John 3:16, Romans 6:23b, Romans 10:13.

Strategy for Witnessing to Someone You Have Known for a Long Time

Sometimes we are afraid to share the Gospel with people we have known for a long time because we are embarrassed that we have never told them how to be saved. How can we tell them that this is the most important decision that they will ever make, and that it is important that they trust Jesus today because they are not guaranteed tomorrow? How can we share with urgency when we have taken so long to tell them? Somewhere along my witnessing journey I picked up a wonderful way to overcome this challenge. Simply begin the witness encounter with an apology. Tell the person: "I need to apologize to you. I have never shared with you the most important thing in my life, and if you will allow me, I would like to correct that today." This breaks the ice for you to then begin sharing the Gospel.

To avoid getting into this situation, as previously discussed, be sure that you are constantly seasoning your words with grace. The reason people get into the above situation is because they never talk about Jesus in their day-to-day lives. If you really love Jesus, if you really are in a relationship with Him, then talk about Him daily. That doesn't mean that you will daily launch into a full-fledge Gospel witness with everyone you meet, but you will set the table for when you do have that opportunity to share the Gospel.

Appendix C
Script for Sharing Your Faith

The purpose of this appendix is to give you a script to memorize as you learn how to share the Gospel using the Bible. While I know that people do not always follow a script, memorizing this will help you know the verses and how to explain them. We will call the lost person you are speaking to in this script John.

Just a note before you jump into the script. Do not be overwhelmed by how long it is. It is very easy to memorize if you first memorize all the verses you are going to be sharing. Once you have the verses memorized, you will see that the script is simply explaining them and is therefore easy to learn.

You: What are the requirements for going to heaven?

John: Well, I think you have to be a good person.

You: So, you believe the requirement to go to Heaven is that you have to be a good person?

John: Yes, that is what I believe.

You: Do you mind if I quickly show you on my phone's Bible app what the Bible says about going to Heaven?

John: Sure.

You: Romans 3:10 says, "as it is written: 'None is righteous, no, not one.'" This verse simply says that there is no one perfect. Everyone has made mistakes and done wrong things. I know I have made mistakes and done wrong things, have you made mistakes in your life and done wrong things?

John: Of course, everyone makes mistakes and does wrong things.

You: Romans 3:23 says, "for all have sinned and fall short of the glory of God." Again, this verse says that we all have sinned and fallen short of God's standard. Sin is where we break God's law. If you've ever disobeyed your parents, if you've ever lied, if you've ever taken something that wasn't yours, then you have broken God's law. I can put my name in that verse and say that "Neal has sinned and fallen short of the glory of God. Can you put your name in that verse?

John: Yes, I could.

You: Romans 6:23a – "For the wages of sin is death..." A wage is something you earn. Imagine you worked all week, and it was pay day, and your boss said: "I don't feel like paying you." Would you be mad?

John: I'd be very mad.

You: I can understand why you would be mad – you earned that money. This verse tells us that when we sin, we earn death. You see, most people think that going to Heaven is about doing more good in this life than bad. That is not what the Bible teaches. The Bible teaches that we must perfectly keep God's law, and if we don't, there is a mandatory sentence – death. Not just physical death, but spiritual death, where we spend eternity separated from God in a real place called hell. If you break a law in this country that has a mandatory sentence, the judge must give you that sentence. It doesn't matter how much good you have done before you broke the law – he must give that sentence. The same is true with God. He has declared a mandatory sentence of death for anyone who breaks His law. As we have already talked about, we are both guilty of doing that. This means that we are both guilty before a holy God, there is a mandatory sentence, and no amount of good works will save us.

This is really bad news, but I'm here to tell you that there is really good news!

John 3:16 – "For God so loved the world, that he gave his only Son, that whoever believes in him should not perish but have eternal life." Even though we have sinned against God, He still loves us. He demonstrated His love for us by sending His only son, Jesus, to die on the cross for our sins. Jesus was willing to take our punishment for us so that we would not have to. Whoever believes in Jesus will not perish but will have everlasting life.

The question is: "What does it mean to believe in Jesus?" Believing in Jesus means to trust in Him. To trust in Jesus, you must stop trusting in whatever you have been trusting in for salvation.

Romans 6:23b "...but the free gift of God is eternal life in Christ Jesus our Lord." Jesus is the greatest gift that the world has ever known. Jesus took the punishment for our sins, and He now offers us the free gift of salvation.

Let me ask you a question: "When does a gift become yours?"

John: When it is offered to you?

You: Can you reject a gift?

John: Yes

You: Then that shows that a gift does not become yours until you accept it. God offers a gift of salvation. If you must pay for something or earn something, is it a gift?

John: No

You: Exactly. A gift is free, or it really isn't a gift. Also, it can be very insulting to try and pay for a gift. Most people are trying to work their way to Heaven. They believe Heaven must be earned, but the Bible says we can't earn it because we are sinners. Heaven isn't a reward to be earned, but a gift to be received. Would you like to know how to receive this free gift?

John: Yes

You: Romans 10:13 "For 'everyone who calls on the name of the Lord will be saved.'" There are four important things to see in this verse:

Whoever – that means salvation is open to all. It does not matter where you've been, what you've done – Jesus is willing and wanting to save you.

Calls – this word means to cry out. It is a picture of someone who is drowning, calling out for help. To cry out for help, you must first realize that you need help. You must confess to Jesus that you are a sinner and ask him to forgive you of your sins and to save you.

Lord – when you call out, you call out to the Lord Jesus. The word Lord means boss. By calling out to the Lord you are recognizing Jesus as the boss of your life. You are now surrendering to His Lordship over you.

Will be saved – when you put your trust in Jesus' work on the cross, then you can know for certain that you are saved! Salvation is not based on our work, but on Jesus' work. We, there, can know for certain that we are saved.

Do you have any questions about what I have shared with you?

John: No

You: Would you like to receive this free gift of salvation from Jesus?

John: Yes

You: You can do that right now. You don't have to go to church or go through any ceremony to receive this gift. You just "call out" to Jesus. You can do that through prayer – which is simply talking to God. I can lead you in a model prayer if you would like to receive Jesus. Would you like that?

John: Yes, I would.

You: Wonderful. Then I want you to repeat this prayer that I lead you in. Understand that these are not magical words. But if they represent that you desire to receive the gift of salvation, then repeat them after me.

(As you lead John through the prayer, do it in small phrases and wait for him to repeat after you).

Lord Jesus, I admit that I am a sinner. I believe that you came and died on the cross for my sins and rose from the grave and I ask you to forgive me and to save me. I also invite you to be the Lord of my life. Save me Lord Jesus. Thank you for saving me, help me to never be ashamed of you.

John, if you just put your trust alone in Jesus to be saved, then you are saved. That means you are a follower of Jesus. Receiving Jesus as Lord and Savior is not the end, but rather the beginning of a relationship with God. You are no longer separated from God because of your sin, but you are now his child. He wants to have a relationship with you and to see you grow as a believer. It is important to read the Bible and get involved with a local, Bible believing church. Can I help you find one?

John: Yes, that would be nice.

Now, let me give you an alternate ending for the script in the instance that John says no to being saved.

You: Would you like to receive this free gift of salvation?

John: I don't think I'm ready.

You: Ok. I don't want to push you to do anything you're not ready to do, but may I ask what your hesitation is?

John: I just need to think about it some more. It is a big decision.

You: I agree, it is a big decision. Let me ask you another question. Let's say tonight you are lying in bed thinking about our conversation and decide that you want to be saved. Can you tell me how to be saved?

John: Um... I'm not really sure.

You: That's ok. I just want to make sure you understand so that you know what to do if you decide to receive this gift. Remember the Bible says to call on the Lord. No matter where you are, you can call on the Lord. Just tell the Lord that you know you are a sinner and that you believe Jesus died for your sins. Ask Jesus to forgive you of your sins and tell Him that you are putting your trust in Him alone to be saved and that you recognize Him as the Lord of your life. Does that make sense?

John: Yes

You: Are you sure you don't want to do that right now?

John: I'm sure, but thanks for sharing with me.

You: Please feel free to contact me if you have any questions or would like to talk about this some more.

About the Author

Neal H. Creecy first surrendered to ministry when he was sixteen years old. He is the Senior Pastor of Redemption Church in Las Vegas, Nevada. He is the Co-Founder and Vice President of Global Church Planting Partners, a mission organization focusing on theological education and church planting  throughout the world. He has trained pastors and church planters all over the United States and the world. Neal has also taught in seminaries in the United States, Africa, and Indonesia. He has done missionary work in over thirty countries. He has had the privilege of teaching evangelism around the world. Neal holds a Bachelor of Music Education from the University of Mississippi, a Master of Divinity and a Ph.D. from Mid-America Baptist Theological Seminary.

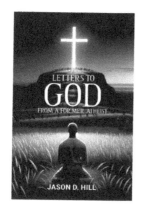